Little People

Little People

Guidelines for Commonsense Child Rearing

Third Edition

Edward R. Christophersen

Westport Publishers, Inc.
Kansas City, Missouri

Text illustrations: David Graves
Cover design: Network Graphics
Cover photography: Eli Reichman
Cover illustration: Mark Walter
Children on cover: Katy Walter, Matt Walter

ISBN 0-933701-32-2

Printed in the United States of America

Library of Congress Cataloging-in-Publication Data

Christophersen, Edward R.
    Little people.

    Bibliography: p.
    1. Child rearing—United States. I. Title.
HQ769.C563   1988   649'.1   88-20789
ISBN 0-933701-32-2

To Miki, Hunter, and Catherine

Contents

Preface   *ix*

Introduction   *1*

GENERAL GUIDELINES   *3*

1. Preparing for Parenthood   *5*
2. Catch 'em Being Good   *13*
3. Self-quieting Skills and Independent Play   *23*
4. Let Them Help You   *29*
5. Monitoring Children   *34*
6. Establishing Orderly Home Routines   *36*
7. Discipline   *43*
8. Lectures and Communication   *54*
9. Modeling and Imitation   *60*
10. Guidelines for Baby-sitters   *64*
11. Divorce   *72*
12. Automobile Travel   *76*
13. Shopping and Other Excursions   *80*
14. Toys   *87*
15. Parents Are Teachers   *93*
16. Television   *96*

COMMON BEHAVIOR PROBLEMS   *99*

17. Bedtime Problems   *101*
18. Toilet Training   *107*
19. Eating Problems   *114*

20. Dressing Problems *118*

21. Bedwetting *122*

22. Thumbsucking *125*

OTHER CONSIDERATIONS *127*

23. Grandparents *129*

24. Exceptional Kids Can Learn Too! *131*

25. Seeking Professional Help *134*

26. Concluding Remarks *137*

Bibliography *139*

Summary Handouts *141*

Preface

Living with children is a gratifying experience. That is not to say that it is always paradise. Children give parents unparalleled joys and sorrows, moments of emotion almost too deep to bear and times of frustration that seem beyond toleration. Parents contribute similar things to children, but parents are also responsible for providing the environment in which the child develops. Most children survive both good and bad childhood infiuences to become normal adults, then parents themselves, and the process begins anew.

In some ways it is remarkable that the process works as well as it does. Children have had no experience in dealing with parents, and most parents have had only limited experience in dealing with children. Even if parents recognize a need for training, there is really very little training available to help them prepare for the practical responsibilities of raising a family. Psychologists, social workers, nurses, and physicians are little better off—most of them have never had one hour (much less one class) of practical instruction in being a parent.

This is not caused by a lack of scientific information on child rearing. Hundreds of researchers have conducted thousands of hours of study and clinical observation and have written hundreds of reports that would bore most parents because they would have no idea how to apply the information from the studies. The work is often published, but the articles that pertain to parenting are mostly speculative, unsubstantiated, or so technical that it is difficult to see how the research relates to parents and children.

Despite this rather pessimistic introduction, a great deal of good work has been done over the past two decades. Many reputable researchers have documented child-rearing procedures that are effective. This good work has been done in small pieces at various places all across the country. The results have often been communicated only among professionals, at meetings and in journals and personal communications. Very little work has examined the implementation of clinical findings in ways that can be used by parents in family environments or by pediatricians in practice.

Most pediatric training programs do not include training in general child-rearing practices. A great deal of time is devoted to training pediatricians in how to recognize and manage every conceivable childhood illness and how to conduct physical examinations on well children, but that is usually where the training stops. Thus, the one health care provider who sees normal healthy children—the pediatrician—may be unprepared to provide guidance to parents for living with their children. Fortunately, many pediatric training programs are now including a little, but very important, exposure to general child rearing.

The aim of this book is to fill a part of that gap. The original version, published in 1977, contained much of what we knew at that time. The second edition, brought out in 1982, added some new information. This current edition, the third, includes a good deal of information that has been identified and evaluated in the last five years. The procedures outlined here were developed in a professional pediatric environment and in a productive research setting that was devoted to work with infants, toddlers, preschoolers, and school age children.

This program provides a comprehensive set of guidelines for parents to follow in living with normal, healthy children and a few suggestions about exceptional children. The procedures stem from the work of literally dozens of clinicians from all over the country. Combining their work into this general program has been a primary interest of mine during the past ten years. During that time, the program has involved thousands of parents and children and has been subjected to rigorous scientific analysis. Over one hundred articles and chapters related to the program have been published in professional journals and books.

Little People is a description of this program written for parents (natural, step, foster, adoptive), nurses, and physicians. One important assumption made here is that parents are obtaining good pediatric health care for their children from the time they are born and dental care from about thirty months of age. Some medical problems can manifest themselves as behavioral problems. Your family physician should be consulted if you suspect that there is an organic cause for the way your child is behaving. Chances are there is not, but it is always best to be certain.

The guidelines in this book are intended to assist parents in day-to-day interactions, and to make child rearing more pleasant—not easier, just more enjoyable. Fortunately, parents can make thousands of mistakes over the years without adversely affecting the development of their child. It's frequently impossible to tell, from one specific situation, whether you handled things correctly. But, over a period of time, you can see by the way your child behaves whether you are doing an adequate parenting job. If you look at the way your child behaves in public and around other people and you like what you see, then whatever it is you're doing, you're doing correctly, regardless of whether it agrees with what you've been told or what you've read.

If, on the other hand, you cannot honestly say that you like what you see when you look at the way your child behaves, then you would be wise to ask "What can I do to improve the way he behaves?" During almost any crisis, it's easy to get upset with your child and attach most of the blame to him. That is one reason it is so important to remember that you can't change the way a child behaves without first changing the way you behave. This doesn't mean that it's your fault when your child does something that really upsets or disappoints you. It does mean that the only way you can alter the way your child behaves is through your own behavior. Laying the law down or giving a lecture is ineffective over the long term, and certainly is unpleasant for you and your child.

Parents have many questions and frustrations during child rearing. Throughout *Little People,* I'll be talking about average, well-intentioned parents and the normal children they are living with. Although many of the recommended guidelines apply to all children, this book is written with what we consider normal children and normal parents in mind.

Living with children is a gratifying experience. It lasts only a relatively short time, then they are gone and raising their own families. But while it lasts, it is a significant part of our lives. This book is meant to help parents get the most out of those years they spend living with the little people they bring into the world and help toward adulthood.

Acknowledgments

Like most authors, I owe a great deal to many persons. My parents made my childhood a pleasant and meaningful experience.

My wife, Miki, my son, Hunter, and my daughter, Catherine, make my days worth living.

The Department of Pediatrics at the University of Kansas Medical Center and The Children's Mercy Hospital have supported and encouraged my efforts to develop a program for working with parents. The Bureau of Child Research at the University of Kansas has greatly facilitated getting the millions of dollars in research grants without which our program never would have been developed.

The development of many of the procedures described here was made possible by a grant to the University of Kansas, Bureau of Child Research, from the National Institute of Child Health and Human Development (HD 03144).

The writing in this book is my own. Many of the ideas came from discussions with my students and my fellow faculty members at the University of Kansas. Practically all the principles in this book stem from the work of individuals noted in the text and from the faculty at the University of Kansas, Department of Human Development—the finest and most dedicated group of professionals working with children, anywhere.

Edward R. Christophersen, Ph.D.
Kansas City, Missouri
May 1988

Introduction

If you are already a parent, you can probably remember the first time your baby smiled at you. It produces an overwhelming exhilaration, one that is difficult to explain, but it's there, it's real, and it's impossible to get any other way. Going into a baby's room when he's asleep and standing there looking down at him (they all look sweet when they're sleeping) is a quite different but equally moving experience. Parents have hundreds of such experiences.

And all parents have some problems with their children. All those children you see jumping around in cars, running up and down the aisles in supermarkets, and spilling food in restaurants belong to someone. And at times they make that person's life unpleasant, if not miserable. Almost every parent who has problems with a child is doing the best possible job of child rearing that he or she knows how to do. Unfortunately, child rearing is something that few parents are prepared or trained for. The chapters that follow are for them—parents who, for the most part, are doing a good job, but want to do better.

A very healthy way to look at your children is that they are little people. By this is meant that they are eventually going to be adults, and you have much to do with both how well they are prepared for adulthood and how enjoyable their adulthood will be. No one in pediatrics or child psychology really knows where to place the most responsibility for the way a child behaves. We know that Mom and Dad have something to do with it. But so do close relatives, neighbors, friends, baby-sitters, day-care workers, and school or preschool personnel. In any event, it's a waste of time trying to decide who is responsible. Your time is much better spent deciding how to develop or maintain appropriate behavior in your child.

The best rule of thumb to follow is that little people should be taught to live by the same rules, scaled down, of course, that big people (adults) live by. Most adults are held accountable for their behavior, good and bad. Many children are not. It doesn't make sense, though, to rear children using standards that don't exist for

1

adults. Adults usually are able to determine whether they're doing what they should be doing. And sometimes adults get in trouble because they break the rules they're expected to live by. Little people break the rules, too, but many times their parents either try to cover for them or try to protect them from the natural consequences of their actions. This is a mistake. You should not rear children as if there were no tomorrow. Some parents say "Jimmy will have enough misery when he's grown up. I want his childhood to be enjoyable." Parents can make childhood enjoyable, most of the time, and still prepare children to be adults.

Many physicians and parents say that a child will outgrow "it"—whatever "it" is. I don't agree with that—parents miss too many good times waiting for their child to outgrow one thing after another. A major advantage in teaching your child how to behave more appropriately is the net result gained: you have more time to spend relaxing with her. Once parents have minimized the time spent disciplining, threatening, and picking up after their child, they find they can do things together that they either didn't have time for before or that they couldn't do because of the way their child behaved. Your list of "things to do with your child" can include (depending upon your values and preferences) anything from going to the park or the library to working on the car. The activity itself doesn't make a great deal of difference—it's the involvement of parent and child that counts. Above all, remember always that parents are *teachers*.

General Guidelines

1

Preparing for Parenthood

Expectant parents can do a number of things before their baby is born, then while Mom is in the hospital with the baby and right after the two of them come home, that contribute to making the adjustment to parenthood easier and more enjoyable.

Selecting a Pediatrician or Family Practitioner

Approximately one-third of the thousands of couples who have attended my childbirth education classes have not arranged for the medical management of their expected child before delivery time. This is not good. There are several excellent reasons for selecting a pediatrician before you deliver, but the main one is to get to know the doctor so you can decide whether he or she is in fact the doctor you want. A doctor who is very good and has an excellent reputation simply may not appeal to some parents. If you find out before you deliver that you do not really care for a particular doctor, you have time to choose and meet another doctor. It is much more difficult to change doctors after the baby is born.

Another reason (in addition to getting good basic medical advice) to schedule a prenatal appointment is to find out how the doctor feels about your child-rearing philosophy. If, for example, you have decided that you want to bottle-feed, but in talking to the pediatrician you chose by reputation you find out that he really does not approve of bottle-feeding, then you might want to consider changing doctors. During this visit you can also discuss such things as when the doctor prefers to switch babies to solid foods or how he or she feels about vitamins, natural foods, and other preferences *you* might have.

An important benefit in having met your baby's doctor before you deliver is that you will know the doctor and the doctor will know you. Your doctor can tell you when and how he or she prefers to have the office notified when you go to the hospital to deliver, and when he or she usually comes up to the hospital to check the baby for the first time. That way, you need not worry about trying to get a doctor to see your baby in the two or three days right after you've delivered. You have the added reassurance that in the event you or your baby should need a doctor immediately, you already have someone you know (and know how to get in touch with) lined up.

In choosing a pediatrician or family practitioner, start by asking the doctor attending you during your pregnancy. You also can ask your friends who they take their children to see. In selecting a doctor you will want to consider some of the following items:

1. Office location and office hours (open Saturdays and/or week nights?).

2. Emergencies—how handled and by whom?

3. Average wait for an appointment, both how many weeks to get an appointment and average time sitting in the office on the day of the appointment. What is the office wait for a well-child visit versus the wait if your child is ill?

4. Auxiliary personnel—how is the office staffed? Who will you see?

During the first prenatal visit to the doctor's office, consider these things:

1. Does the doctor or nurse take a good medical and social history? Does the doctor ask questions about both mother and father's past health and the health of both families?

2. Is the office clean and neat enough to suit your tastes?

3. How adequately does the doctor or nurse answer your questions?

4. Is the doctor willing to explain treatment options or alternatives when appropriate?

5. What are the doctor's fees? For what?

6. Specifically, what kind of training does the doctor have? (The person who answers the phone can usually answer this question and save you the embarrassment of asking the doctor.) Don't be afraid to ask if the doctor completed his or her residency (advanced medical training in pediatrics received after medical school). This line of questioning is meant to determine whether the physician is a

board certified (or board eligible) pediatrician or family practitioner—if so, then his or her credentials have been carefully screened by
qualified medical peers, which is an important consideration.

7. If it's a group practice, how many doctors are in it? What are
your chances of always seeing your doctor? For routine phone calls,
who can you expect to talk to about your child? If this is a nurse,
what is his or her background and training (formal or on-the-job)?

8. Do you like the doctor and the staff? Do you think you can
depend on them?

After the prenatal visit, the parents should talk about whether
this is the doctor and the office they want to trust to take care of their
baby. If it is, then follow the doctor's advice. If not, schedule a prenatal visit with another doctor to make a comparison.

Buying for Babies

Most expectant parents know what things they will need to purchase prior to their baby's birth and shortly thereafter. However, the
only authoritative source previously available to parents that presented objective information on everything from cloth versus dispos-
able diapers to car safety seats was *Consumer Reports.* The same pub-
lisher now publishes a book called *Guide to Baby Products,* which includes objective evaluations of baby foods, diapers, gates, and portable cribs, for example, as well as advice on how to buy a variety of
items for babies. The *Guide* can be purchased directly from Con-
sumers Union. Most parents will get more information from the
magazine and/or the *Guide* than from child psychology books that
have few practical answers to common questions.

Educating New Parents

Most hospitals offer, through their obstetric nursing staff or obstetric or pediatric nurse practitioners, education for new parents in
infant caregiving, which includes instruction in bathing, diapering,
feeding, and dressing. New parents, regardless of their educational
backgrounds or socioeconomic class, should receive this kind of instruction. You feel much more confident after having a nurse dem-
onstrate the procedures, then practicing with the nurse there and
having time to master these caregiving skills before going home.

Unfortunately, this teaching is usually done by the day shift,
which may leave out fathers with daytime jobs. To leave out the

baby's father is a mistake. Infant attachment or bonding begins immediately and is helped along by regular physical contact with the parents. Fathers who receive instruction in infant caregiving procedures are much more likely to continue to give care when mother and baby come home. A common complaint from mothers is that fathers don't help with infants, but it's easy to understand a father's reluctance if he hasn't been taught what he needs to know.

An alternative to instruction by hospital staff and frequently the new mother's only choice is for *her* to teach her partner how to care for their child. This is really asking for it. Most married persons have experienced the frustration of trying to teach their partners something. Generally it is better for the father to spend time with the nurse, too, until he knows how to handle his baby and feels confident in doing so. This knowledge of caregiving skills will increase the likelihood that the father will have contact with his child, which will in turn facilitate the bonding between the father and the child. A father who enjoys caring for his infant helps reduce the mother's workload.

Although the vast majority of new or expectant parents have a great deal of curiosity about living with and caring for an infant, there aren't many books on the topic written specifically for them. A companion volume to *Little People,* the *Baby Owner's Manual,* describes infant caregiving and developmental behaviors for the first year of life and answers typical questions on establishing routines, buying car seats, and so on. Most new parents find it useful to have such a handbook at home for reference after leaving the hospital.

Grandparents and Relatives

When you're expecting, you should remind persons who are kind enough to offer to help during the first week or two after the baby arrives that you *want* to take care of your baby and the biggest help would be for them to take over mundane household responsibilities such as fixing meals and doing laundry and dishes. A grandmother often comes in and immediately begins taking care of her grandchild (because she is experienced), leaving the mother and father to take care of the household chores. This not only can antagonize the parents, it postpones the inevitable learning process that comes with caring for a baby. Why not let the parents get started immediately with learning and bonding?

Many grandmothers have attended my childbirth education classes with their sons or daughters, and several have commented afterwards that they had never thought about their actions like this before. They just assumed that they could provide the greatest help by taking care of the baby. These grandmothers also have said that letting the parents get used to their new baby made perfectly good sense. In fact, I've never had a grandmother at one of these classes disagree with this notion, although they have been known to disagree with me on other issues!

Infant Caregiving

There are several simple things, in addition to the actual physical acts involved in taking care of a new baby, that help you get used to each other. One is that you should talk to your baby while you are taking care of her, in normal adult speech, not silly baby talk. Talking to a baby tends to have a soothing effect on her, gets her acquainted with Mother's and Father's voices, and provides her with examples of adult speech. There's no sense in using baby talk. It's not necessary, it's not particularly becoming, and it doesn't provide a sound basis for later language development. Parents also should begin reading to their child long before the child has any understanding of what is being read. From children's bedtime stories to the evening newspaper, the baby doesn't know the difference, but the repetition of adult speech over the first several years can do wonders for the child's own speech development.

Another important thing to do is to spend time playing with your new baby. This doesn't mean playing catch. It means spending time exploring him. While feeding your baby, examine his fingers and toes, stroke his hair, or simply hold one of his feet. These gestures, again, have a soothing effect on your baby and facilitate bonding between the two of you. The most important thing for parents to do with their newborn (and up to adolescence) is to have a great deal of brief, nonverbal, physical contact. Recent research has shown that this quiets babies as well as helps them to grow. This is even true for babies who are born prematurely and who spend the first few weeks or months in an intensive care unit. The babies who receive adequate amounts of physical contact gain weight faster, though they do not necessarily eat more, they leave the hospital sooner, and they have a lower total hospital bill.

These activities are both soothing to your baby and enjoyable to you. They serve another primary function—they make caregiving more enjoyable, and the more enjoyable it is, the more you are going to do it. That's just plain human nature. This process, then, tends to have a snowballing effect: the more time you spend pleasantly interacting with your child, the more pleasant the child will be to interact with.

You should try to develop standard caregiving routines and, within reason, stick with those routines. For example, it's a good idea to use the same place and the same procedures when diapering a baby. This should be a place that is safe for your baby and one that has all of the necessary items in easy reach. The reason a routine is important is twofold. One is that you will become proficient more quickly, which makes caregiving less of a chore. The other is that as your baby becomes accustomed to the routine, he will fuss less during that routine. For example, many newborn babies will cry while their diaper is being changed. This is unnecessary—as the diaper is being changed, he certainly doesn't need to communicate that his diaper needs attention. Crying is one behavior that some babies exhibit or engage in too much and that too many parents accept as inevitable. Most parents, perhaps through instinct, learn to read their baby's signals, and crying is almost always read as a distress signal. If you must listen to crying through every diaper change, you begin to wonder what it is you are doing wrong, and eventually, through frustration, you conclude that your child is just very difficult to care for. This is very definitely to be avoided! It is possible that you have not established a routine, so your baby doesn't know what to expect next. If you use the same routines each time you engage in a caregiving activity, and this results in your baby crying less, then you are doing it right.

Preparing for a Second Child

Though much has been written about first babies, not so much is available about preparing parents and existing children for the arrival of a new baby into the home. Here are a few points to consider:

1. The less your toddler's life is disrupted by a new baby, the less he will resent the baby. If you have had special times with your toddler, preserve these. If you've been saying prayers and talking for a

short time at bedtime, arrange your schedule so that you can continue these activities uninterrupted. Young children really seem to prefer consistency in their schedules and activities. Either keep things the same or change them before the new baby arrives.

2. Try to make whatever physical changes you plan to make at least one to two weeks prior to the birth of the new baby. If you are going to change bedrooms, or switch from an infant car seat to a toddler car seat, or from a feeding chair to a feeding table, make these changes prior to the arrival of the new baby. If you do discuss these changes with the toddler, make the discussion very brief, firm, and don't blame the new baby for the changes.

3. Examine how and when you discipline your toddler and decide if you need to increase or improve your disciplinary procedures. If any changes seem necessary, begin to make them at least two weeks before the new baby is due. If the changes are made ahead of time, the toddler/preschooler will not associate them with the new baby—which is the way you want it to be.

4. Don't talk to your toddler if he wakes up during the night with the baby. Provide him with a lot of physical contact, rub his back, pat him, or just hold him gently, but try to keep your mouth shut. If you can make these nighttime meetings brief and quiet, he will stop waking up with the new baby. If, on the other hand, you get into the habit of spending fun times with your toddler in the middle of the night, he will come to enjoy them and you will find them very difficult to stop. Night feedings with the new baby should be brief and boring. The only purpose for these feedings is nutrition, so keep them like that. When your newborn awakens at night, go in immediately, pick her up, feed her, change her, and place her back in her crib. Do not turn on any lights. Do not talk to the baby. Try to make these nighttime contacts as brief and matter-of-fact as possible, with a lot of physical contact.

5. Do not begin toilet training your toddler within 90 days of your expected due date. If you are not sure, don't begin the process. There is little to be gained by toilet training early and a lot to lose. Generally, it takes about six months after toilet training before accidents are completely eliminated, so don't expect a newly trained toddler to go accident free.

6. If you have someone in your home to help you after the new baby is born, ask them to help with the house first and the toddler

second. The baby's care is best left to Mom and Dad.

7. Many parents will bring a present for the toddler when they bring the new baby home from the hospital. This is probably okay— it gives the toddler a nice introduction to the new baby.

8. If you have friends who have always paid a lot of attention to your toddler and they come over to see the new baby, ask them to begin by paying some attention to the toddler. That way she won't feel so much like she's been replaced by the new baby.

9. Many parents worry that their toddler will suffer when Mom is gone from the house for a couple of days to have the baby. The only real difference, if the toddler stays with her Dad, is that the child might eat the same food and wear the same clothes for the entire time that Mom's gone. This is usually because Dad just isn't used to having so much responsibility for the toddler. Fortunately, whatever happens during these few days isn't going to make much difference in the long run. And, for those dads who haven't had a lot of contact with their young children, the couple of days that Mom is in the hospital can be just enough to establish a new, special relationship, which can continue for a long time.

10. As soon as you bring the new baby into your home, begin teaching your toddler how you want her to treat her baby brother or sister. Whenever she is gentle, touches the baby, or talks to the baby, give her lots of love pats. Conversely, whenever she is rough with the baby, discipline her immediately (more information on disciplining toddlers comes in a later chapter). Do not, however, lecture her on how to act with the baby.

2

Catch 'em Being Good

The most important rule in living with a child is to have a great deal of brief, nonverbal, physical contact with him when his behavior is neutral or acceptable—not just when you feel like it and not just when he is doing something praiseworthy. The more effort that is expended on neutral and acceptable behavior, the less effort you will need to devote to punishment and the happier everyone involved will be. A lot has already been written about the need for verbal praise with children. However, many parents have already found out that verbal praise will interrupt whatever their child is doing. Brief, gentle, nonverbal, physical contact, in the form of pats on the head, back, arms, and legs, is much better than verbal praise with young children because it is much less likely to interrupt them. Many infants and toddlers, when praised, will stop whatever they were doing. The nonverbal physical pats usually just interrupt children at first. As you get better at using it, this kind of contact will not interrupt them.

You can be nice to little people when they're good, just like you're nice to adults when they're good. We all know of examples where adults have done something good and not heard a word about it, like the wife raking the yard only to have her husband not notice. Or the husband getting his hair cut or washing his wife's car and not having her be pleased. When adults put forth a special effort and it's not noticed, they are disappointed. What about little people? They're not even certain that what they did was right. *Every time you miss a chance to catch your child being good, you miss a chance to teach him how you would like him to behave.* If you do this very often, don't be surprised when he doesn't know what you want him to do. You must teach him, and the best way to do that is to catch him doing it the way you want it done and provide him with brief, gentle, nonverbal, physical pats. It is important, and this will be covered in detail further on in this book, that your child receive a great deal of this kind of physical contact whenever he is doing something that is all right with you.

Infant (birth to 12-15 months)

One of the first things new parents learn is that infants cry a lot, more than they ever dreamed a child would cry. How do you reduce a child's crying without stifling her? When you first bring a baby home from the hospital, it doesn't take long to notice that she seems to go spontaneously from a sound sleep to loud crying. However,

after she's two to three months old you'll notice that she will wake up and just look around her crib, making babbling or cooing noises before she starts crying. If you'll get up after she wakes up but before the crying starts, you can catch her being good (in this case, playing nicely in her crib). In this way you can teach your baby that when she wakes up, if she'll just play a little while, you'll be in in a minute to get her up, feed her, and change her diaper. If you do this, you'll quickly discover that your baby cries less when she wakes up.

Note, also, that if you should slip up several days in a row and wait until the baby cries before you go in to get her, then you're back to teaching her that if she wants you to come in to get her, she'd better start crying, because otherwise you won't get up. I'm not saying that it's bad for babies to cry. Crying serves useful purposes—like letting moms and dads know that babies are uncomfortable, hurt, or hungry. What I am saying is that *you* will be a better father or mother if you don't have the feeling that your baby cries all day long. We all know that it's easier to do a good job at something we like to do. Taking care of an infant can be a truly delightful and pleasurable experience if you like to do it. But excessive amounts of crying, when your baby is not in distress, can quickly dampen the joys of early parenthood.

One of the biggest mistakes that parents can make with infants in the second and third month of life is to always "help" them to get to sleep. Well-intentioned parents will nurse their baby to sleep or hold and rock her to sleep, then carefully place the sleeping baby in her crib. In this way, the nursing or the rocking becomes the *transition behavior* that the baby uses to get to sleep. If Mom is breast-feeding the baby to sleep, then the breasts become the baby's *transition object.* Later on, if the baby should wake up in the middle of the night, she will look for and need this transition behavior in order to get back to sleep. Because Mom is the one with the transition object, or because the baby isn't capable of getting out of her crib and over to the rocking chair by herself, it becomes almost impossible for the baby to get herself back to sleep.

If, however, you make it a practice to put your baby to bed awake but sleepy, she will learn her own skills for falling off to sleep. Further, should she awaken during the night, she will be able to get herself back to sleep. Any parent who helps a baby get to sleep both for naps and for the evening, but who expects the baby to "cry herself to sleep" in the middle of the night, is going to get very, very frustrated. In effect, you are teaching your baby transition behavior during the day that you don't want her to use during the night. Don't confuse your baby and frustrate yourself. Put your baby to bed awake and leave her alone long enough for her to learn her own transition behaviors. (A chapter dealing with sleeping problems in more detail follows later in the book.)

Toddler (12-15 months to about 36 months)

Toddlers present a new challenge to parents. They move around the house and get into almost everything, but they have little knowledge of how to use the things they get into. This is a time when children have a tremendous amount to learn, but they usually aren't willing to wait until one of their parents is ready to teach them. Besides, many parents of toddlers still haven't learned that you can't teach a child through the lecture method. (An entire chapter is devoted to this later in the book.) I've heard many parents say, "If I just didn't have anything else to do, I'd be able to keep up with Jeanny." Mom tries to go ahead with her work, ignoring Jeanny as much as possible in an effort to get everything done in one day. Jeanny in turn just roams around, pushing and pulling on things, trying to see what makes everything work—which is all very appropriate. Unfortunately, Mom (or Dad) continues to ignore Jeanny so long as she doesn't do anything wrong or get into something she's not supposed to get into.

So what's Jeanny learning? *As long as you behave yourself, Mom and Dad will ignore you. If you want their attention, you'd better create an unusual noise, like something breaking, dropping, or falling over, then they'll be right there.* Rarely do parents intentionally ignore a child until she does something wrong, it just works out that way. Dad is busy (sometimes with important things like reading the paper or watching television), so he doesn't notice what Jeanny's doing until she does something drastic. A classic example of this sort of situation involves the mother or father who is talking on the telephone—most will ignore a child who is watching television or playing quietly. But just let the child get into something that he's not supposed to and parents interrupt their phone calls in a second.

If, on the other hand, Dad changes that situation just a little bit, he can teach Jeanny some of the things he wants her to do and at the same time continue to watch the news or read the paper or talk on the phone. Suppose that Jeanny comes over to Dad's chair carrying a magazine in her hand. Every parent knows that magazines aren't sacred to toddlers. And parents also know that you can't hide every magazine that comes into the home, so why not use this situation to begin teaching Jeanny what magazines are all about? If she sits down on the floor near you and puts the magazine in her lap (it doesn't matter if it's upside down and backwards), lean down for two seconds and touch her on the head or back.

The point is that Jeanny should get attention from you whenever she does something appropriate for her age. Nobody expects a toddler to sit down and read aloud from an encyclopedia, yet when she approximates this by sitting down and turning the pages of a book or a magazine, many parents don't see the connection between turning pages and learning to read. This is not to say that if a child learns how to turn pages, he or she learns to like to read. The point is that children can be taught that sitting down (for even twenty seconds) with a magazine in their lap is enjoyable, not because there's some kind of kick from holding a magazine, but because Mom or Dad likes it and lets them know it. If on 300 different occasions, Jeanny sits with a magazine, turning the pages, and on many of those occasions Mom or Dad gives her a brief "love pat," Jeanny will learn to enjoy sitting and looking at a magazine. Mom and Dad are then well on their way to teaching Jeanny one of the thousands of things she has to learn.

If you see your daughter petting the dog gently, go to her and give her a love pat to let her know that she's doing something you like. She'll learn that you like for her to treat the dog kindly. You should, of course, discipline her if she mistreats the dog (discipline is covered in a later chapter), but it's unlikely that you will teach a child how to do something right by disciplining her when she does it wrong. If you discipline her when she mistreats the dog, she may learn what you don't like, but she isn't learning how you want her to treat the dog. The same thing is true if you find your toddler playing nicely with her brother. Let her know, with love pats, that you notice—by doing so, you teach her how you want her to behave. All of the to-do several years ago about the importance of TLC (tender loving care) in rearing children was on the right track; the advocates just failed to point out that *when* you deliver TLC is as important as *how* you do it.

No one in his right mind would suggest that you should pick up a child and cuddle him right after he's knocked a lamp over, telling him what a good boy he is and how much you appreciate his breaking that lamp for you. But, there are less extreme examples of giving TLC at the wrong time. Let's say that you're in the kitchen fixing dinner and David gets too close to the stove, so you spank his hand. Then you feel sorry because you spanked his hand so you pick him up and love him. Unfortunately, through instances like this, particularly if you haven't been too good about catching him being good, David learns that if he wants to get your attention, he has to do something wrong first, then get a spanking, then you'll pick him up and love him. Why not start out by giving David lots of *feedback* (love pats) to show him that you appreciate what he's doing?

With the example in the kitchen, if David is at the kitchen cabinet where you store most of your pots and pans, and he's taking them out one at a time and looking at them, then setting them on the floor, give him love pats—make it clear that what he's doing is all right. He's better off playing with pots and pans than putting his hands on the stove. If he gets too close to the stove, remove him from the area of the stove. In this way, David learns both what you want him to do and what you do not want him to do. He also learns that it is fun to be in the kitchen with you when you're preparing dinner.

Preschooler (36 months to 5 years)

Giving your daughter love pats when she's working on a puzzle or looking through a book is a beautiful way to encourage pre-academic behavior. It is much more difficult to try to teach her in some formal fashion all that she needs to know in order to read. Many of the prerequisite skills and much of the initial enjoyment of reading are best taught to your child over an extended period of time, primarily by making certain that she knows you understand and appreciate her early attempts. Your daughter, in fact, doesn't even need to know that what you're doing today is directed at encouraging her to enjoy reading at some later date.

Many parents punish their children for not studying. Some force children to study. If a child has no appreciation for studying and has not learned the skills used in studying, forcing him to spend a certain number of minutes each day at a desk is a waste of time.

Why not avoid the hassle completely by just letting your preschooler know that you like to see her reading her book? You'll find that your daughter soon comes to enjoy reading. That shouldn't come as any surprise if you've been working on catching her reading. If you begin early to work on the skills that are later used in studying, you can be assured of a good start in making her entire educational process easier for both of you.

School Age (5 years to puberty)

Much of what I've said about "catch 'em being good" relating to infants, toddlers, and preschoolers has become second nature to successful parents by the time their child is in school. School provides literally hundreds of opportunities for parents to let children know that they like what they're doing, made easier because school-age children have much better language skills.

Dinner time, for example, can be a source of enjoyment for the entire family if children are encouraged to talk about what they did in school that day or what happened in some after-school activity. The same principles about catching them being good apply, even if you're doing it automatically. If a child is relating how he is almost finished with his next project for Cub Scouts, or how her ballet teacher said she was doing much better in her practicing, then the parents have a constructive, pleasant conversation going and the children will profit from it.

All the parents need to do is to prompt their child (by generating discussion) to talk about the good things that happened during the day. If, on the other hand, the child is encouraged to talk about how he beat up Pete or gave Susan a judo chop, and the parent thus makes it very clear that he did an acceptable thing by hurting someone else, then the parent can expect to hear more of the same and less about the kind of behavior a child needs now to succeed in school or later on the job.

In fact, it's frightening how much influence parents have over children's behavior. If a parent really does find it enjoyable to talk about "who beat up whom," I cannot tell them that they are wrong. I can tell them, however, that they can expect to see more of whatever kind of behavior they themselves engage in and whatever behavior they encourage their children to discuss and engage in. A parent who encourages discussion about fist fights should not expect a child to try to change the conversation over to how well things are going in school.

A related issue here is that this is the age when a child begins to find out how he relates to, and fits into, a universe bigger than just his family. If a child comes home from school and tells his parents what a rotten job his teacher is doing—how he or she is always yelling at and picking on people—the parents' response should be quite guarded. If the parents immediately agree that the teacher doesn't know what she's doing and ought to be replaced, the child may decide that he was completely justified in whatever it was that he did wrong. Worse than that, the child will be on his way to learning that he doesn't have to follow the rules at school because "My Dad will get me out of it."

Teachers, like parents, generally do the best job possible under the circumstances. To assume immediately that your child is right and the teacher wrong is probably a mistake. You have to consider that, in addition to trying to be good teachers, teachers have had a lot more training at being teachers than parents have had at being parents. I'm not saying that teachers are always right, only that they should always be given the benefit of the doubt. Even in cases where the teacher is wrong, the parent would do well to use this as an opportunity to point out to the child that the world isn't always fair, and that there are many occasions when a person is going to know that he is right when he's accused of doing something wrong. There are always better ways to handle unjust situations than with violence or threats of reprisal.

Catch 'em Being Good

This phrase, to the best of my knowledge, first appeared in Wesley Becker's 1971 *Parents Are Teachers: A Child Management Program*. The point is that children like to do things that gain recognition from their parents. If most of a child's attention comes from inappropriate or obnoxious behavior, then regardless of his age or the kind of attention he gets, that child's actions are likely to be inappropriate or obnoxious. On the other hand, if a child earns recognition from socially acceptable behavior, then she is more likely to exhibit socially acceptable behavior.

Notice, too, that I have tried to stay away from giving concrete examples of what is "good" and what is "bad" behavior. For one child, helping Dad feed the cows is appropriate; for another, it's reading the encyclopedia. In some contexts, learning how to defend oneself on the way home from school is necessary, although even for those children there are constructive behaviors they need in addition to self-defense. The social and cultural setting in which the parents live determines, to a certain extent, what is acceptable behavior.

Regardless of what behaviors parents select to teach their children, catching them being good is one of the best and most effective ways to teach them. If children are expected to assist in serving appetizers at an evening cocktail hour, they should receive some recognition from their parents when they perform well. If the children in another family are expected to be on their best behavior when Mom's boyfriend is at the apartment, she should remember that they need positive feedback, even though she's primarily interested in entertaining her boyfriend. Parents enjoy being around their children when the children are behaving in ways the parents think is appropriate. To ask from parents, then, a little extra effort in praising or encouraging their children for behaviors that the parents enjoy is reasonable.

A brief word of advice on catching children being good: there's no reason to spend a long time doing it. It's much better to catch 'em being good many times a day with brief love pats than to catch them only once a day and spend fifteen minutes expressing your appreciation. A child's attention span isn't long enough for him to listen to anything for fifteen minutes. Besides, when you're talking, it's difficult for your child to learn much, except perhaps that you want him to be quiet when you're talking.

Don't let yourself get trapped into thinking that "since Jimmy's being quiet, I'd better not disturb him." As rationales go, this is a loser. The first few times you catch 'em being good, most children will act a little surprised and some may even stop what they're doing. What this tells you is that you haven't had much experience with catching 'em being good or it wouldn't be so disruptive.

Doing things that make your child feel proud certainly comes under the heading of catching her being good. An example of this would be displaying schoolwork that was well done (you don't have to spend time bragging about the work, just be sure that someone notices it and says something). Another form of encouragement that can make another child feel proud is what I call "third-hand compliments." If Mom tells Dad what a nice job Scott did on a school project or how well he behaved at the Little League game, both Dad and Scott will feel good about it.

Some caution should be exercised when praising accomplishments to another person. Be careful not to push your children into participating in activities they don't enjoy. Some boys enjoy playing baseball, but they don't get nearly as wrapped up in the games as their parents do. This takes some good judgment on the parent's part. Be sure your child knows you're proud, but don't use him to fulfill your own needs.

As we've been discussing "catch 'em being good" we've also been talking about what we call "time-in." Time-in is very important in raising children and will be discussed in the chapter on discipline—there we talk about "time-out," which simply refers to taking away your time-in. Some examples of how time-in is expressed are love pats, talking, walking, reading, touching, sitting together, facial expressions, and third-hand compliments.

3

Self-quieting Skills and Independent Play

In the grand scheme of things, two sets of skills will make an enormous difference with your child, depending on the extent to which he masters them: self-quieting and independent play. Almost inevitably, when parents say that they have a "difficult child," the child hasn't developed very good skills in these two areas.

When a baby is less than a month old, a test called the Brazelton Neonatal Behavioral Assessment Scale can measure a lot of different behaviors, reactions, and skills that babies are born with (that aren't learned at that age). One of the most important of these, to parents, is what Dr. Brazelton calls "self-quieting skills," which refer to a child's ability to quiet herself down when she's fussing or crying. In the newborn period, babies with good self-quieting skills are the "easy" babies. They are the infants who seem organized and content—the happy ones. We used to think that babies either had good self-quieting skills or they didn't, and there was nothing that a parent could do to improve the situation. Now we know that there are several things that parents can do to improve a child's self-quieting skills.

The previous chapter on catching children being good discussed transition objects and how children could better quiet themselves down at bedtime if they had a reliable transition object. This discussion was about self-quieting skills and gave examples of transition objects that an infant could use to promote self-quieting. There will be literally tens of thousands of occasions besides bedtimes in your child's life when he will be upset or unhappy about something that he cannot or should not do anything about. If you can prepare him for how to deal with these times, you'll have taught him some very valuable skills. Conversely, if you get into the habit of always helping (that is, taking over) your child during these times, not only will you have the frustration of always needing to "bail out" your child, he will have the handicap of never learning self-quieting skills.

Infant

In infants, the best example of self-quieting skills is seen when they are trying to go to sleep at naptime or bedtime. Children with good self-quieting skills go to bed, make some cute noises, entertain themselves by sucking on their hand or rubbing a blanket across their cheek, and, within a short time (and without any help from an adult), they are asleep. What they have learned, and this is extremely important, is how to relax when they don't necessarily feel like relaxing.

There are three major components to going to sleep: the infant must be tired, in a subdued or quiet environment, and relaxed. It's relatively easy to make sure that a baby is tired—just give her many opportunities during the day to use up energy. For an infant two to three months old, just holding her head up while lying on a blanket requires a lot of energy. As babies get older, attempts at crawling and rolling over or bouncing in a walker also require great effort. What doesn't really require much energy is to be carried around most of the day by your mom or dad.

Many parents think they are doing the best for their infants by entertaining them for hours on end. Actually, while it is important to spend such time entertaining and stimulating infants, it is equally important to make sure that your baby has time to herself when she can learn to explore and manipulate her environment. Lying on a blanket looking around the room, reaching for and playing with a ring of keys or a teddy bear, involves exercise and is mentally stimulating to an infant. While they may not have the skills to do this when first placed on the blanket, over a period of weeks infants can get very good at keeping themselves busy.

What may be difficult for some parents to appreciate is that this kind of independent play is excellent for an infant. As your baby moves his hands and sees his mobile move, he begins to engage in more purposeful interaction with his environment. Sometimes you can watch an infant push a mobile over and over, dozens of times, watching it intently all the while. He is learning, ever so gradually, that he can have an effect on his environment. With time, he also learns that he can have an intended effect on his environment. Through independent play children learn which of their behaviors have what effects on their environment. Before an infant can begin to learn independent play, though, he must be able to self-quiet.

When I recommend specific activities to reduce your child's crying, it is to teach her self-quieting and, in time, independent play. Reduction of infant crying, in and of itself, has little value. There are some doctors who recommend, in an effort to reduce infant crying, that mothers carry their infants in a cloth pouch for hours every day. Not only is this potentially dangerous (if the mother should fall forward, the entire weight of her body would be forced against her baby), but it reduces crying without teaching either self-quieting or independent play. When parents can provide their infant with lots of love pats for independent play, they are not just reducing crying, they are making it possible for the child to explore and learn about the world around her. Parents cannot do this for babies by carrying them around, explaining or naming everything for them; babies learn how their environment reacts to what they are doing through experience.

Toddler

By the time a child reaches toddler age, the absence of self-quieting skills is not only very obvious, it becomes a real handicap. A child playing on the floor with building blocks is not just stacking blocks—he is learning how to impact his environment. As children become more and more proficient at independent play, they learn to compare their mental images with what they are actually doing in their environment. For example, when a toddler is building a garage for his trucks, he has a mental image of what the garage should look like, probably based on one he's seen or that Mommy has built for him before. If the child should discover, after his project is completed, that the truck does not fit in the garage, he must learn both to make the walls higher and to revise his mental image. It is this revising of mental images that makes up the valuable learning experience—the learning experience that cannot be done *for* him, but must be done *by* him.

The use of "time-out" for discipline (a concept that will be developed in detail in a later chapter), as well as "time-in" for independent play, leads directly into more time spent in independent play, one of the most beneficial activities a young child can engage in. Every time a child is placed in time-out until she is quiet, she is learning self-quieting skills. Every time that she receives love pats for playing nicely by herself, she is learning independent play skills. Obviously, playing with a parent or another child is beneficial and helps to promote forming and revising mental images, but independent play is the one activity that contributes the most toward comparing mental images with the environment. The toddler with poor self-quieting skills and, consequently, poor independent play skills, is at an obvious disadvantage over peers who have these skills better developed.

Preschooler

By the time a child enters preschool, she has many opportunities to engage both in social play and independent play. The fussy child who only stops fussing when entertained by an adult is already operating at a handicap. Although preschool teachers cannot always verbalize why, they may tell parents that their child is very distractible and requires close adult monitoring. This is often, if not usually, due to the child's lack of skills for independent play.

The older a child is when you begin working on independent play, the more difficult the task. The challenge is not just that she *hasn't* learned independent play, it's that she *has* learned that adults will entertain her if she fusses long enough. Thus, parents really have a choice: you can work at teaching your child independent play skills that she can use throughout adult life, or you can teach her to be almost entirely dependent upon adults for entertainment and stimulation. Unfortunately, parents often find that being the entertainer is the easiest thing to do—it keeps the child busy, and then parents can convince themselves that the child is learning a lot from the interaction because her vocabulary grows rapidly.

School Age

Perhaps the most frustrating activity that parents encounter with school age children is homework. For the parent who has relished the role of entertainer/stimulator, homework presents real difficulty. The teacher usually tells the parent that the child needs to work on his homework alone, so that he will learn not only the material but also the process by which the learning takes place. Ironically, the children with the most homework often are the ones who don't have sufficient independent play skills to do their work when they are at school. Hence, the inability to function independently catches up with the child and causes problems both at home and at school. Not only do these children lack the necessary independent play skills, they have been taught to depend upon adults for their structure.

Most teachers, if given the choice, would prefer to have children in their classrooms who are well behaved, with good self-quieting and independent play skills. Conversely, most teachers also dread the opposite: the child whose skills deficits disrupt both teaching and learning in the classroom.

Self-quieting and Independent Play Skills

Many parents just take child rearing one day at a time, with no master plan and no long-term direction to what they're doing. These parents accept immediate gratification in lieu of long-term gains. While there's a great temptation to reduce a child's whining and crying by almost any means available, if this is done at the expense of self-quieting skills and independent play skills, the cost to the child is significant.

Parents can begin during infancy to encourage their child to explore and learn about his environment by himself. You must resist the temptation to help at every opportunity, bearing in mind that what you do today has strong implications for what your child will be willing and able to do tomorrow. Maintaining this effort up through the toddler, preschool, and school years helps your child acquire the skills for functioning independently in their growing world.

Ironically, the people who are the most productive on their own are usually also the ones who contribute the most to a group's efforts. Groups of almost every kind depend in large part for success on the individual contributions of their members. While the group process is important, it cannot and does not transcend the individual efforts of the individuals who make up the group. Every successful meeting usually represents the fruition of the efforts that the participants put in since the last meeting. All of us have worked with adults who "talk a good game" but are very disappointing when it comes to actually getting something accomplished. These are almost always grown up little people who never learned the skills for getting things done themselves.

4

Let Them Help You

Parents can actively draw children into "everyday living" by letting them help with a variety of household activities. Although this can be a little difficult at first, it is much better for you to let them help than to turn them away. Most children enjoy helping their parents around the house, and they can learn a great deal while doing so. Although the "helping" might be only simulated work in your vicinity, it's good to have your children nearby and feeling "in sync" with you.

Because the idea is for the child to see you doing something well that you enjoy doing, I don't suggest that a father or mother start out on "let them help you" with a job that he or she finds barely tolerable. If Dad absolutely hates to put snow tires on the car and usually loses his cool before he's finished, then by all means he shouldn't start out by having the children help change tires. The same goes for ironing, bundling newspapers for the recycling center, or whatever else you find yourself doing that you really don't enjoy.

Find jobs that you enjoy and that don't present an obvious risk to your child's safety, then have him help you in any way he can. The help needn't actually be constructive. In fact, with younger children, the help might actually slow you down. That doesn't make any difference. Until a child learns how to help, you should expect him to be a slight hindrance. As he gets used to being around when you are working (and learns that it's pleasant to be around you when you are working), you'll find that he'll imitate what you do more and more. (A later chapter focuses on modeling and imitation.) Letting a child help you, especially a younger one, requires a good deal of patience before you see the fruits of your labors. But a cardinal rule to follow is *never* to yell at or ridicule your child when he's helping. In fact, there is *no* situation in which I'd recommend ridiculing a child. When a child is trying in his own way to help you, the last thing you

29

want to do is make the experience unpleasant for him. Helping affords an excellent time to "catch 'em being good," no matter how far you have to stretch your imagination to see what he's doing as good.

It takes time for children to learn complex skills. Many tasks involving complex skills should be broken down into smaller, more manageable pieces to make the learning easier. Asking a child to do the dishes is asking too much if she doesn't even know what "doing the dishes" means. It's far better to do the dishes yourself while encouraging the child to help you. Notice that I said *encouraging*. This can be done simply by saying something like "Oh, thank you for bringing your plate to the sink. That makes it much easier for me to do the dishes," instead of "Come on now. Quit poking around. Get the rest of those dishes over here." Besides, talking nicely to your child is much more pleasant for both of you. Who cares if Johnny brings only his plate the first couple of times? The goal is to get Johnny to the point where he is able to do the dishes by himself, which of course takes some time. Some age-appropriate examples follow to help clarify what is meant by "letting your child help you."

Toddler

One very common situation where a toddler can help is in picking up toys. Toddlers are always taking toys out of whatever you put them in. Notice, I didn't say that they play with them—just that they take them out. When you're putting the toys back in the toy box, simply encourage Jennifer to help you by saying something obvious like, "Help Mommy pick up Jennifer's toys." Don't be surprised if Jennifer doesn't help you the first few times. She might even work against you by taking the toys out as you're putting them in. So what? The aim is to interact pleasantly with Jennifer while *you're* doing a job. Sooner or later Jennifer will make a move that looks like she's trying to help. When she does, catch her being good. It doesn't have to be much, just a love pat or a smile. Pat her on the back. Jennifer is soon really helping you pick up her toys. You certainly shouldn't expect perfect performance the first couple of times, and it'll be ages before she's doing it without being asked. What's important is that Jennifer is helping, in her own little way, and you are recognizing it and making sure she knows you appreciate it.

You can apply the same thing to something like feeding the dog. Yes, that's right—toddlers can help feed the dog. They can point to the dog food container when you say "Let's feed Andy" or just accompany you when you feed the dog. And while they're helping you, you have the opportunity to make certain they know you appreciate the help.

Preschooler

Because preschoolers get around so much better than toddlers, they can help a great deal more. For example, before you start mowing the yard, a preschooler can help by removing rocks and sticks from the path of the lawnmower. Although at first this may really be mostly rearranging rather than removing, given encouragement and time, the results will begin to look like what you would have done yourself.

All too often one parent says to the other something like "Will you take Scott with you so I can clean the house?" or "Will you keep Scott in the house so I can clean the garage?" What's poor little Scotty supposed to do while you're doing all the important jobs? If parents took both those suggestions, Scotty wouldn't help either in

the house or in the yard. Most preschoolers will be around for a long time, so you may as well get started early in your job of teaching them how to help you. That does not mean that Scotty should always be allowed to help, but at least one-fifth of the time. The only way Scotty is going to learn to be a real help is by letting him help when he's little and giving him lots of praise and encouragement.

It's surprising how much children enjoy helping their parents. There's something heartwarming about watching a preschooler really working hard to please his mom or dad. At this age, children still haven't learned to cover up when they are enjoying something. A small child asking his mom to "check my room" after he's spent ten or fifteen minutes picking up his things can look so proud. It's a look we don't often see on adults' faces, probably because they rarely experience that kind of wholesome pride in these days of plastic clothing and fast food.

School Age

When children reach school age, they can do all kinds of things around the house, but their parents must acknowledge that they are capable of doing these jobs. A school-age child can help clean the house, the yard, or the garage. I keep emphasizing "help" to stress that it's fun for children to help Mom or Dad. It's not quite as much fun for them to do a job completely by themselves. As children get older, there are more and more things they can do by themselves. The important thing about helping on a job is that it provides a rich opportunity for pleasant parent-child interactions. While dusting and straightening the living room, you can talk to your son or daughter (or both) about all sorts of things that interest them.

This is really what professionals are talking about when they say that parents have to "communicate" with their children. Remember that communication isn't even remotely related to interrogation or nagging. It isn't something you have to make an appointment for or plan for days ahead of time. A parent and child can communicate very naturally about all sorts of things while they are working together. You'll find that it's much easier to communicate with your growing children if you start doing so when they're young. This approach is much better than waiting until a child is having difficulties. At a time like that, you may not be really trying to communicate, not in the sense that you want to find out how another person (children are persons) feels about things. What you may be doing instead is trying to get your child to help you figure out where you went wrong. That's a question only you can answer— don't burden your child with your soul searching.

Let Them Help You

A word of caution is necessary here. If you have not previously been allowing (allowing, not forcing) your child to help you, you may find that he is resistant to the idea. So what? Many adults are resistant to new ideas. Just take time to encourage your child to help you and he will. He'll come around, especially if you don't force him.

I think that a parent's most important job is being a teacher. If you, as a parent, are spending all of your time doing jobs around the house while the children sit around like kings and queens watching you or the TV, you are missing wonderful opportunities to communicate with your children while doing jobs together. Equally tragic is the fact that you won't have the time to do things together away from the house if your time is wholly spent doing home jobs. If children help with the routine jobs around the house, then you will have more time to spend together. Even if you spend the time just talking, it's time spent interacting. I have heard parents say that they really didn't pay much attention to their children when they were growing up. I hope persons who make statements like that aren't really serious. It is an absolute pleasure to watch children grow and develop, and no parent should miss any part of the process.

Parents often comment that they can't wait until the day their children do things because they want to or because they know they need to be done. These parents are really asking "Why should I have to keep reminding them? Why can't they do it because it needs to be done?" The answer is simple. You have to remind your children to do things until you teach them to do things without your reminder.

5

Monitoring Children

If your daughter is playing quietly in the family room and you are in the kitchen preparing dinner, don't wait for her to get into trouble before you leave the kitchen. To do so teaches her that if she wants you to stop fixing dinner for a minute, she'd better do something you don't like. Instead, periodically stop whatever you're doing (very briefly, as in catch 'em being good; only ten or fifteen seconds are necessary) to check on her.

A good way to decide how often to check is to estimate how long she usually goes without getting into trouble. For example, if she usually goes ten minutes on a task or a series of tasks before getting bored and getting into trouble, you should check on her after about eight minutes so you can catch her while she is still being good. In this way, you'll be pleasant and encouraging instead of having to discipline her. Once you come up with a monitoring time that usually catches her still behaving nicely, you can increase the time between checks by a minute or two each week.

You should be careful not to disrupt activities when you're monitoring. At first, even five seconds of attention may be disruptive, but this will change within a week and you can come in, give your daughter some brief love pats, and leave, and she'll act as if you didn't appear. Don't be misled by this. She knew you came in, and she loved it. The idea is to have many short pleasant interactions with your child, and in order to do this, you may have to monitor activities quite frequently at first.

Infant

Most parents start off as good monitors with infants, usually checking on them very frequently to see that they're not too warm or too cold. I suggest that parents carry over this initial monitoring for physical well-being to cover the behavioral development of their

34

child. One real advantage of checking on an infant is that infants are almost always "cute" and appealing, and frequent checks serve to strengthen whatever bonds are already developing between parent and child.

As soon as your infant begins to react to the environment, by playing with a mobile or reaching out for toys, you should begin to stimulate him. A periodic, reassuring voice, a smile, or a soft touch lets your infant know that you are there and that you care.

Toddler

Toddlers require almost constant monitoring as they ramble about the house or apartment. They're learning about the world they live in. As you check on them you can help them learn by giving them feedback. Many parents find themselves carrying on one-way conversations with their toddlers as they go about their household chores. They're almost constantly saying things like "That's nice," "Do you want to go?", and "Oh! that's pretty." These pleasant inter-actions are all the more important because your toddler is beginning to find out what your house rules are and hence will encounter disci-pline for the first time. The contrast between the normally pleasant interaction with a parent and what is experienced when a rule is broken serves as a valuable teaching experience.

Preschooler and School Age

For both these age groups, monitoring combined with catching them being good educates your child in the ways that you want him to behave. As your child gets older, the need for monitoring lessens, but it should never be dropped completely. Monitoring is part of the way you teach your child, and your teaching job continues until the day he leaves home.

Monitoring Your Children

Keep in mind that you can't teach your young children any-thing unless you are frequently checking on them. The old notion that you should "leave him alone—he's quiet" is ridiculous. If he's quiet, check on him. If he's behaving appropriately, give him a love pat. If he's doing something that's against the house rules, discipline him. None of this is possible, of course, unless you put out the effort needed for effective monitoring.

6

Establishing Orderly Home Routines

If you accept the basic premise that parents are teachers, then it makes sense to establish consistent and orderly home routines. An ideal teaching situation in a classroom involves a pleasant atmosphere in which a child practices something over and over again, receiving feedback from the teacher until the task is done right. For example, when children are learning the ABCs, their teacher may have the class practice several letters repeatedly. The teacher does not expect the class to learn all twenty-six letters in one day and isn't surprised when a particular student has to practice each letter many times in order to write it correctly. A teacher doesn't usually shout at children when they make mistakes and certainly would not spank them for writing letters improperly. These same guidelines used by teachers in classrooms can be used by the teachers at home—the parents, YOU!

I hope that I have sold you on the value of letting your children help you. Teaching your children to help you is a prerequisite to establishing orderly home routines. If you let your child help, if you remain reasonably calm, and if you provide constructive feedback about her progress on the development of a particular skill, then you can expect dramatic gains. Learning takes time—time for the skill to be practiced and practiced and practiced.

Orderly and consistent home routines greatly facilitate a child's home learning. The younger the child, the simpler the rules. But regardless of the age of the child, the rules can't be changed from day to day or from moment to moment—not if the parents expect the child to progress. If you want your daughter to hang up her coat when she comes home from school or from a shopping trip, then you must require that the coat be hung up *every* time she takes it off.

If you require your daughter to hang up her coat only twice a week, two things will happen. One is that she will never get into the habit of hanging up her coat when she takes it off. Second, you will lose your temper more often when you do attempt to enforce the rule. Debbie will come home three or four days in a row and throw her coat over a chair. The fifth day she comes home and throws her coat over that same chair, you come unglued. You get trapped into saying things like, "How many times do I have to tell you to hang up your coat?" or "I'm not going to tell you again to hang up that coat." Sorry, but if you had followed the guidelines discussed so far, you would know what to do in this situation. You, as parent and teacher, must check whether Debbie hangs up her coat every time she takes it off (monitoring), and every time she hangs it up properly, you should catch her being good. To be certain that she knows how to hang up her coat properly, you can try practicing hanging up the coat. (Let them help you.) When you're straightening up the living room, Debbie can help you by hanging up her coat and you can give her immediate feedback that she did it correctly. The answer to the question "How many times do I have to . . ." can be answered very simply—until you, the teacher, teach her that you want the coat hung up every time.

The more consistent and orderly you are in following the rules you make for your children, the better your children will behave and the less you'll need to rely on discipline. Much discussion and arguing can be avoided by having, within reason, orderly and predictable routines. You should decide on reasonable bedtimes for your children (certainly there are exceptions to this) and stick to it. If you want to teach your children to go to bed when you tell them it's time to go to bed, you have to follow through every time you tell the children to go get ready for bed. If you allow your children to change their bedtime by whining and fussing, then you're teaching them to whine and fuss instead of teaching them to go to bed.

Decide what jobs the children can do. You'll be surprised how much children can do if you give them a chance! Remember that your most important job is that of a teacher. Don't use all your time and energy being maid, cook, and disciplinarian. Let your children do whatever they're capable of while you spend your time teaching them how to do the various jobs involved in running a home.

If you establish orderly and consistent home routines and make it a point to catch the children doing well in their respective jobs, you'll find that your home is a much more pleasant place in which to live, for both you and your children.

Infant

In order to establish an orderly routine for an infant, you should decide how you want something done and then consistently do it that way. For example, if you're bottle-feeding your baby, go through the same sequence of behaviors each time you bottle-feed her. Go into her room, pick her up, carry her to the kitchen, place her in her infant seat, and hold her so you can look at her face and begin feeding her. You'll find that at first your infant usually cries until she gets the nipple into her mouth. However, as she learns your morning feeding routine, she'll begin to calm down before she actually comes into contact with the nipple. At first, you can expect her to calm down when you're looking at her with the bottle in your hand. Later, she'll calm down when you place her in her infant seat, and still later she'll calm down when you pick her up from her crib—because she's learned (because you've taught her) that when you pick her up from her crib in the morning, she's going to get fed almost immediately.

The side benefit from establishing orderly routines for infants is that they fuss and cry much less. Starting the morning out pleasantly can make your whole day look better. On the other hand, starting out the day with an infant screaming while you try to get her bottle ready has an upsetting effect on most mothers and fathers that sometimes lasts into the later part of the day.

Toddler

It's also important to establish morning routines for toddlers, particularly if you have more than one child. If you want the mornings to get off to a good start, then you must teach your children what you expect of them and then catch them when they're doing it correctly. Toddlers can't really help you a great deal in the morning, but they can do a lot to upset this time of day. Many times after you've placed your toddler in his high chair, giving him a piece of toast while you prepare the rest of breakfast will, if used consistently, keep him happy for the time it takes you to get things ready. He'll learn that breakfast always comes shortly after he gets his piece of toast, so he'll probably fuss less. When shopping for a high chair, consider buying one of those that look like a card table with a seat in the middle; they make cleaning up much easier.

The toddler age is the time to start teaching your child how to dress himself. This doesn't happen overnight, but if you start on some of the basics early, then you're much less likely to end up with a four- or five-year-old who can't dress himself. The way to do this is to teach each little step in getting dressed as if it were a skill all its own. As you pull a shirt over a toddler's head, many parents will say, "Where's Eddie? Where's Eddie?" while the shirt is covering his eyes. Then you pull the shirt down and say, "*There's* Eddie." Gradually, you let Eddie do more and more of the pulling, so that eventually he's doing most of it. You can do the same thing when putting his arms through his shirt sleeves and his legs through the pants legs. Each of these separate skills has to be learned before Eddie can dress himself. You may as well get started early so he'll have acquired some of the skills alerady when he begins trying to dress himself. Many of these skills are prerequisites to others. Pulling pants up and down, for example, is absolutely necessary before a child can be toilet trained.

Preschooler

At this age, children can start doing more things around the house by themselves. Many preschoolers are in the final stages of learning how to dress themselves, how to pick up their rooms, and how to make their beds. Don't forget that they have to be taught how to do all of these things. Just the simple requirement that Dottie make her bed before she can have breakfast can result in Dottie's bed being made every morning. She may not do it like you'd do it, but then there's no satisfaction involved and no opportunity to catch her being good when you make her bed for her. Preschoolers can start to learn how to carry their silverware or dishes to the sink after eating. A little person has to learn how to do it someday, and the younger he starts, the easier it'll be (within reason, of course).

This is also a good time to begin teaching the table manners you want your children to use. It's a very simple matter to require your children to say "please" and "thank you" at the dinner table. When they ask for the potatoes, all you have to do is say something like, "What's the magic word?" You'll be surprised how quickly they learn that they get the potatoes when they say "please." Don't allow yourself to be conned by your child saying that he didn't want the potatoes anyway. If that's what he says, fine. Don't give him the potatoes. It doesn't take too long before he'll understand that you have a new rule and that he must say "please" when he wants something.

Two additional points need to be made here. One is that it won't do you any good to sit down and explain to your son the importance of good table manners (more about this in the chapter on lectures). If you want him to say "please" and "thank you," require it. No discussion is necessary. What is necessary is that he have many, many opportunities to see that saying "please" gets the potatoes and failing to doesn't. The second point is that you just might want to try saying "please" and "thank you" yourself. There is no good reason why children should be required to say "please" and "thank you" when their parents don't. When your child starts consistently saying "please" and "thank you," don't forget to acknowledge that you appreciate his good manners. Something like, "You asked for that nicely. Here are the potatoes" will suffice.

School Age

When children are in school, much of their time *has* to be orderly and predictable if they're to get to school on time each day. Some parents allow themselves to be blackmailed when the child gets up in the morning and dallies around instead of making his bed or getting dressed. Then it's time to eat and Mom doesn't want to send him off to school on an empty stomach because everyone knows that isn't good for a child. Neither is it good for a child to con you into straightening up his room and dressing him. Fortunately, a child can easily survive three or four mornings in a row without breakfast while you're teaching him an expected routine. It takes more than four missed breakfasts to cause malnutrition, but that is usually all it takes to teach a child to straighten up his room in the morning.

Remember that you need to catch 'em being good. If your son starts making his bed, tell him that you appreciate the fact that he started right away. Don't expect him to complete the bed the first time. If you want him to start making his bed and he does, then you have an ideal opportunity to catch him being good. Because he learns that you appreciate the fact that he even got started on his bed, you're on your way to having him do it every morning. If you begin

by waiting for him to make the bed completely, though, you may have a long, long wait.

When you first get started on a job like making the bed, it's probably best to require it seven days a week until your child is doing a good job of making it every day. No sense giving him days off before he's learned how to do the job correctly and has had lots of opportunities to practice his new skill. If for some reason you don't particularly want the beds made before school, you could make a rule that the beds must be made before the children can play after school or watch television. Or you might not even care whether your child makes his bed, which is okay too—so long as you don't make the bed for him!

Getting Along

If you haven't done this already, you might also want to start working on how your children get along together. Make some clear-cut rules about how Johnny can and cannot treat his little sister, then stick to those rules by giving him attention when he's being good with his sister and by disciplining him when he isn't.

Child's Night Out

When the members of a family are getting along well together, the children usually enjoy going places and doing things as a family. Parents are often at a loss as to what to do or, alternatively, do the same two or three activities over and over again. One option for deciding on how to spend the evening is what we call "child's night out."

Every week or two, parents should plan to spend an afternoon or an evening with their child(ren), with the child allowed to choose, within reason, what the family does. If the child chooses, for example, roller skating, the parents would take him to a roller rink, put on skates, and skate with him. Don't be surprised if your child picks an activity that he enjoys but that you may not be really good at; just keep in mind that he is choosing an activity that he wants to share with you. Over time, you will probably notice that you really enjoy your child's night out because you are doing something as a family.

The Benefits of Orderly Routines

One concern that most readers probably feel by now is that these guidelines (on the surface anyway) sound as if they must take an incredible amount of time to put into effect. But those who are parents already know that it takes an incredible amount of time to rear children. I'm merely suggesting that you spend your time teaching them instead of just getting from one day to the next. Being a parent is both an awesome responsibility and a tremendous pleasure. By following the guidelines, each day should get a little more enjoyable (if not any easier) and your children should become better behaved. Because you spend so much of your time with your children, establishing consistent, orderly, and predictable routines will make your lives together more pleasant and more rewarding. All children require a great deal of time and attention. By managing the way you give that time and attention, you become an effective teacher as well as a caregiver, while the amount of time you invest remains the same. Quite often you even gain time to spend together in games or excursions outside your home.

There is something associated with this kind of learning that we don't hear about enough from the experts. In our work with adolescents who have been in trouble with the juvenile court, we find that most delinquents do not regularly participate in any *structured* activity. They don't engage in sports, they don't work on school projects, they don't go scouting, camping, hiking, or the like. Children in serious or repeated contact with the juvenile court rarely engage in any recreational activities with either of their parents.

Waiting until a youth is in trouble with the court to make your first attempt at doing things together is a big mistake. Once a young person has the habit of roaming the streets or riding around in automobiles, it's very, very difficult to change. Make your life and your children's lives more interesting—encourage structured activity and constructive use of leisure time from early childhood on. Don't wait until a juvenile court judge tells you that you must do more together. It may be too late then. Your opportunities to catch 'em being good may be all gone.

7

Discipline

Although much has been written about disciplining children, my view on the subject is somewhat different from most. I believe that parents need to think more in terms of how to teach their child to behave in a manner that is acceptable to them—not in terms of what to do when he doesn't behave acceptably. Discipline, of course, is important, but much, much more so is teaching a child to behave the way you want him to behave. It might help to remember that big people don't get spanked every time they make a mistake. Why should little people?

First of all, discipline and enforcement of discipline should be as unemotional, low keyed, and matter-of-fact as possible. A rule is broken (not just bent) the very first time your child breaks it. Allowing her to break a rule three or four times just teaches her that it's all right to do whatever the rule forbids some of the time. When your child breaks a rule, she should pay for it in whatever way you enforce broken rules. Notice *she* should pay for it, not you. When you get upset and huffy, you're paying for the rule violation just as much as your son or daughter is, and you cannot be an effective teacher when you're upset. The two just don't go together. In fact, you simply give your child a poor example of what to do when he gets upset. If there's a single mistake that parents make with discipline, it's that they wait too long to do it. The longer you wait, the more likely you are to get upset and the less your child will learn from the discipline.

Second, the more unpleasant the discipline is to the parent, the less likely it is that he or she will use it. That's just human nature, so pick a form of discipline that doesn't automatically result in your not wanting to use it, like spankings, for example. Later I'll describe a form of discipline (the chair) that usually doesn't upset parents, or children for that matter, but that is effective just the same.

Third, once your son or daughter has been disciplined for a

broken rule, no part of the incident should ever be mentioned again. If you want to talk about it again, just wait; chances are he'll break the rule again and you can discuss it then. Most rules will be broken several times (if not dozens of times) before your child learns them. If you go into a minor rage each time a rule is broken, you'll probably be exhausted before your child learns the rule. Your job is to teach your child constructive things. Blow ups only serve to teach your child that when he's upset he should go into a rage because that's what you do.

Children learn by doing things and then getting feedback on what they've done. This usually has to occur many times before a child learns what you want him to learn. So, when a rule is broken, enforce it and then drop the matter. Any carrying on after a child has paid for a broken rule is unpleasant for both of you and has no teaching value whatsoever. It's a waste of time and energy, tends to upset you more than you were about the rule violation itself, and makes you a less effective teacher.

Developmental Discipline

One very important consideration in any discussion of discipline with children is that the discipline must be geared to the developmental level of the child. Probably the most common mistake that parents make in trying to discipline young children is assuming that young children can benefit or profit from discussions about their behavior. Nothing could be further from the truth. Children below the age of ten years do not have the cognitive ability (the brains!) to operationalize conversations with their parents. In English, that means your attempts to discuss your child's behavior with him are an absolute, utter, and complete waste of time. When you tell a toddler to be careful with his baby sister, he may be able to repeat back to you, "Baby, careful," but that doesn't mean he's able to follow through on it. When parents spend a lot of time trying to reason with their children, they begin to have false expectations that the children have somehow benefited from these conversations. Afterward, when the child still doesn't follow the rules, parents become frustrated and angry, feeling much of the time like their child is purposely defying them.

The effect on the child is even worse. When a parent spends time verbally reprimanding a child or trying to identify why she insists on behaving the way she has been, the child gets one and only one message—her mom or her dad doesn't like her. Think about it. Young children don't have jobs, spouses, or children. The only thing that they have to think about is themselves. When one or both parents are reprimanding or trying to reason with him, all young Ethan gets out of it is that his mom is mad at him. Many parents have experienced the sequence of reprimanding a child, the child saying "Mommy, I'm sorry. I won't do it again," and then minutes later seeing the same behavior over again. The parents then repeat their admonishment, and the child feels even worse. Over time, the repeated attempts to reason with a young child only serve to lower his self-esteem.

Spanking does the same thing—it lowers children's self-esteem. Spanking is not effective teaching; it is much better to have your child sit on a kitchen chair for three or four minutes (but never more than five minutes, no matter what the child did and no matter how old he is). There is only one way a child should earn a spanking—by getting up from the chair before his time is up. If he gets up, spank him once, and only once. Remember, the first spank is for the child (teaching) and all the rest are for you (revenge). Don't be reluctant to have your child sit on a chair ten or twenty times in a single day if he deserves it.

If you use the chair correctly, without a series of preliminary warnings, you will find that you won't be giving any more spankings. We call the chair a "time-out" chair because it's a time when your child doesn't get pleasant verbal and physical interaction with you—his "time-in." It's the contrast between time-in and time-out that makes time-out effective. If you stop the time-in, though, then there is no such thing as time-out.

A distinct advantage in using the chair for discipline is that it's much easier on your nerves. Most parents can't spank a child without getting somewhat upset themselves—which, as mentioned previously, only serves to lessen the chances of disciplining the child in the future. The nice thing about the chair is that it gives both parent and child a chance to cool off for a few minutes before they interact again.

A very handy item to buy to help keep track of the time your child spends in the chair is a small portable timer. (Not the one on your stove, unless your stove is portable.) When you first begin to

use the time-out chair for discipline, go through a couple of "practices" when the child hasn't done anything wrong and no one is mad at anybody else. Tell your child one time what the rules for time-out are. Begin by saying that he must sit in the chair quietly before he can get up. Ask him then to try it out by sitting on the chair. After he's on the chair for two or three seconds tell him that he can get up. Try this several times so that he can begin to get the idea that being quiet is one of the most important things if he would like to get out of the chair.

Starting off with these "practice sessions" and then using very brief time-outs for the first day or two will make discipline easier for parents and children. After that, you can begin to gradually lengthen the time spent in time-out—from three seconds of quiet, to five seconds, and so on. After a few more times, lengthen the quiet period required at the end of time-out to ten seconds, then twenty seconds. After a couple of days of practicing, the time can be expanded to several minutes.

Always wait for your child to be quiet before you set the timer. Never let a crying child out of time-out for any reason. In fact, we say that a child can urinate, defecate, vomit, and bleed and we won't let him up until he's quiet. You can explain once (if your child is at least three years old and of normal intelligence), briefly, that if he gets up from the chair he will get one hard spank on his bottom, be placed back in the chair, and the time will start only after he is quiet. If you spank your child only for getting up from the chair, and if you use the chair for all other rule violations (even the big ones), you'll be surprised how rarely you have to spank your child. Once they learn to sit in the chair and "do their time," you'll find that disciplining your children is much easier. It becomes matter of fact, and you'll be doing much less yelling, spanking, or vainly trying to reason with them. The chair should become a quiet time for both you and your child.

In conjunction with using the chair, and this is very important, I recommend that your child be relaxed and over any upset before getting up from the chair after a time-out. For example, after Jamie is sitting quietly in the chair, set the timer for three minutes. (A rule of thumb is a *maximum* of one minute for each year of age—a three-year-old gets three minutes, a two-year-old gets two minutes. But no child, regardless of how old, should ever have to be in time-out for more than five minutes *after* they are quiet and relaxed.) If she makes too much noise, cries out, calls for Mother, or gets up before the three minutes run out—start the timer again. After she has been quiet for three minutes and the timer rings, go over to her, place your hand gently on her back, and tell her it's all right to get up now. If she says "No," or cries again, or looks at the floor and acts angry, set the timer for three more minutes. The reason for this is that you don't want Jamie to get up if she's still angry or in a bad mood. She will just end up in the time-out chair again, and you run the risk of getting angry with her in the process.

Nothing should be mentioned about the time-out once the timer bell has rung and the child has been told that she can get up from time-out. While many parents are tempted to tell their child that they "don't ever want to see that type of behavior again," this is really just exactly the wrong approach to take. Children learn much faster if they are given many opportunities to practice whatever it is we want them to learn. If you put your daughter in time-out five, six, or seven times in a row for the same misbehavior, she will learn the rules much faster than she would if she only broke the rule a couple of times a year.

Whenever your child is sad over one of your house rules, it's perfectly all right for her to go to the chair and have a good cry. Although a parent should not stifle a child's expression of legitimate displeasure, you should not have to pay for your child's misery and woe. If you feel it is necessary to discuss a house rule with your child, *do not* do so right after the rule has been broken and the child has done the the time-out. Wait at least fifteen to thirty minutes or until your child has begun to do something that is acceptable to you, whichever is longer, before you even attempt to discuss the time-outs with her. This waiting period usually results in both a parent and a child who are no longer interested in discussing either the time-out or the behavior that got the child placed in time-out. The parent is no longer angry at the child and the child no longer has anything to gain from discussing the time-out.

I've been asked by parents as well as professionals if I would ever recommend spanking. The answer, and one that has been re-affirmed for me over and over again, is that most parents already spank their children. They don't have to be taught that. What they need to learn is an alternative to spanking that works as well (the chair), and how and when to spank when they do decide to spank (only once, only when the child gets up from the chair). I honestly believe that most parents can raise their children without ever giving them a traditional spanking.

Infant

Until a child is able to get around on his own, the responsibility for his safety rests completely with his parents. An infant shouldn't be placed near electrical outlets, hot radiators, or other dangers. For an infant who isn't able to move around, discipline is out of the question. Disciplining an infant for crying is ridiculous. As mentioned in the discussion of "catch 'em being good," there are numerous ways parents can reduce an infant's crying without compromising the care she is receiving. Becker and Becker offer a very nice discussion of this in *Successful Parenthood: How to Teach Your Child Values, Competence, and Responsibility*, which was published in 1974. What they suggest, and I agree with, is that when a crawling infant starts to get into something that you don't want him to get into, say "No," pick him up, and move him to something that's all right for him to play with (his toys, for example). Spanking an infant before he is old enough to know the rules is a waste of time. When an infant constantly gets into something, it's an indication that he needs more attention when doing things that you allow him to do or he needs more to occupy him (toys, stuffed animals, etc.).

Toddler

With young toddlers, it usually isn't necessary to use the chair. Simply remove the child from whatever he's doing and place him on the floor in another room. If he comes back crying, do it again. He'll soon learn that when he's full of misery and woe he must go into the other room and sit for a minute.

My preference is to place the toddler in his playpen, then walk away. As soon as he is quiet for five seconds, go back in, pick him up, and take him back to where all the action is. If you set a time requirement that's too long, it will be a very long time before the toddler meets it. With a young toddler, five seconds of quiet is all that is necessary to get across the idea that you won't pick him up while he's still crying. It's unrealistic to expect an unhappy toddler to go to his playpen and be quiet for four minutes, so don't expect it.

You needn't be concerned that your child will learn to fear the playpen. If children always are relaxed before they leave the playpen, they will come to associate going there with relaxing and will actually get better at calming themselves down because they are learning self-quieting skills. The same point can be made for parents who choose to use the child's crib for time-out. If the child learns to associate the crib with relaxation, then he will learn to relax more quickly as he gets more practice with time-outs in the crib. When the playpen and the crib are used correctly, children do not come to fear them, nor do they learn to avoid them.

There is a descriptive chart at the end of this chapter showing time-out for toddlers (using the playpen) and regular time-out (using the chair). Most of our rules for the use of time-out are included in these guidelines.

Preschooler

The chair procedure was developed with preschoolers and works best with them. Some children will try very hard to make you think that going to the chair doesn't bother them a bit. Good. The procedure wasn't developed with torture in mind. Just let them sit there looking as if they enjoy it. Take my word for it—they don't like sitting in the chair. But if they can convince you that it really doesn't bother them, then perhaps they can get you to switch to something that isn't nearly as effective.

Be sure that your child cannot see the television set from the chair, and try to pick a place where he can't be a part of what's going on around the house. Notice that I did not say the child should be placed in a corner, bathroom, or closet—that would be inhumane. The chair works much better if the child can hear the rest of the family having a good time. While the child is in the chair, no one should be allowed to speak to him or interact with him in any way, not even to remind him about the rules for getting out of the chair. Do not use the child's bedroom for time-out. When a child is in time-out he should be able to see you, see that you are not angry, and see what he is missing. This isn't possible if you send him to his room.

School Age

School-age children don't like to sit in a chair either, and hence the method is effective with them also. We have used the chair successfully with children up to age fourteen. Beyond that, it depends on what kind of control the parents have over the child. For older children, the only method we recommend when the chair doesn't work is "job grounding," which is discussed in detail later. The one form of discipline to avoid is sending your child to her room. A child's room should remain a private place where she can go to be alone, to read or daydream or whatever; don't ruin that by using the room for discipline.

If the older school-age child is a major problem to his or her parents, chances are the family needs a special program or professional help beyond the scope of this book.

Discipline

A crucial point in this discussion is that discipline, by itself, is notoriously ineffective in teaching children how you want them to behave. All you can hope to accomplish with discipline is to teach a child the things that you *don't* want him to do. In the absence of teaching him the things that you *do* want him to do (catch 'em being good), discipline alone will not get the results you want. As a rule of thumb, you should strive to catch your child being good ten times for every time you have to discipline him. Obviously there are some days when this is impossible, but it's a good goal.

If you find yourself spending an inordinate amount of time disciplining your children, you are probably neglecting to catch 'em being good. This is a very serious mistake. Overuse of discipline tends to result in a snowball effect—more discipline leads to more inappropriate behavior. This is a very unpleasant position for parents and children to be in. The only way to get out of it is by working very hard to accentuate the positive, to make time-in more pleasant.

The answer to the often-raised question "When should I begin disciplining my child?" is quite simple: "When he starts breaking your house rules." Age-appropriate discipline, as described in the preceding sections, begins with the infant and continues right on into adolescence. The age-appropriate disciplines are listed below:

Age	Discipline	Time	Explanation
Infant (7-15 months)	Crib or playpen	5 seconds of quiet	Very brief
Toddler (15-36 months)	Other room or chair	Maximum of 3 minutes quiet	Brief
Preschool (36-60 months)	Chair	Maximum of 5 minutes quiet	Brief
School Age (5 years to puberty)	Chair	Maximum of 5 minutes quiet	Brief
	Grounding	1-3 jobs	Brief

Grounding as a Form of Discipline

With older children, above seven or eight years of age, time-out should remain the first form of discipline that you usually try. However, there are some times when just placing a child on a chair for a couple of minutes simply doesn't seem like a severe enough form of punishment. Our rule of thumb is that, whenever you begin to search for a stronger or more severe form of punishment, you should first examine the amount and type of time-in that you have with your child and do everything you can to strengthen this positive interaction. Given that time-in is really good with your child, there are still occasions when a more memorable form of discipline is appropriate. In these cases we recommend the use of *job grounding*.

I invented job grounding because the more traditional time-based grounding just doesn't work like it's supposed to. When a parent grounds a child for a month, the child usually stays grounded for one month whether his behavior is beautiful during that time or horrible. Job grounding, though, controls for these excesses. The child is forbidden to have any privileges (such as talking on the phone, having friends over, watching television, or eating dessert or snacks) until he has completed some assigned jobs. For example, if your son should be caught riding his bike up to the shopping center without permission, then he might receive a two-job grounding. That means that until he has finished his two assigned jobs, whether he completes them in twenty minutes or in two weeks, he is completely grounded. (There is a written handout on grounding at the back of this book.)

Many times parents aren't certain whether or not to be sympathetic when they discipline a child. They often confuse sympathy with lenience. Parents need not worry about showing genuine sympathy for a child's predicament. If your child wanted to go bowling on Saturday morning but was grounded in the morning and couldn't get his job done in time, don't say "You've been rotten all week and I'll be darned if I'll let you go bowling. Not over my dead body!" Instead, you could say, "I know what you're going through. I'd hate to miss bowling when I'd planned on it all week long. I hope you never miss bowling again because you were grounded." Sympathy, in this brief form, is appropriate so long as you don't give in. Teaching a child isn't easy, and there will be times when being a teacher will make you uncomfortable. Don't let this discourage you, though— it's part of being a good teacher.

There are several mistakes that parents with children of all ages seem to make with regard to discipline. One, they wait too long to use discipline. Every time that you allow your child to get away with a behavior that you find objectionable, you are actually encouraging her to engage in that behavior again. Two, every time that you warn your child about a behavior, you are actually encouraging the child to engage in that behavior again. Three, every time that you make up excuses for why your child engaged in a certain behavior, you are encouraging her to engage in that behavior again. Four, many parents give entirely too many commands. Do not give your child a command unless you intend to follow through with it all the way up to and including time-out. Five, many parents give a command when they don't care whether it is carried out immediately. If you allow your child to wait for television commercials before getting ready for bed, then wait for the commercial before asking him to begin. That way, you don't get caught by the child asking if he can wait until the commercial.

Probably the most important point to remember about discipline is that much of what we, as parents, want our children to learn cannot be learned if they aren't at least reasonably well behaved. Art appreciation, sports, and foreign language study all have an element of self-discipline that is almost essential to their completion. By beginning to teach your children to follow simple verbal commands at young ages, and continuing to expect a respectable level of compliance on up through childhood, you are actually doing a lot to prepare them for the world that they will enter by the time they complete their formal education. I have never talked to a teacher or to an employer who looks for and recruits undisciplined individuals for their settings. The child who is reasonably, fairly, and unemotionally disciplined by his parents learns to accept discipline as a part of life—which is the way it is for most adults.

8

Lectures and Communication

Lectures belong in lecture halls, not in homes. Do not lecture your child—not even if you think you are reasoning with him. Threats and nagging are useless in dealing with children and they tend to upset you more. If anything, threats make children behave worse, not better. Whenever you catch yourself saying "If you do that again . . . ," you are threatening your child. Parents often warn their children time after time. Needless to say, this "perpetual warning system" doesn't work. But more importantly, when you're threatening children you're not teaching them how to do something correctly.

At times it is difficult to remain completely calm after a child has done something that really upsets you, but threatening him isn't going to make him behave better. The relief a parent feels when he or she threatens a child is temporary. Whatever was done to upset the parent will usually be done again, much to the parent's dismay, and will be followed by more threats. Even threats that are followed by discipline are not nearly as effective as teaching your child the proper way to behave.

When a child commits some forbidden act for the umpteenth time, this situation should provoke some genuine parental soul searching, to discover how to best teach your child whatever you want him to learn. Frustration is a very real emotion that seems to demand action, but in order to be useful, energy at a time like this must be directed toward figuring out what teaching should be done. (Reminder: do the soul searching while away from the child.)

Talking *with* your child, not *at* him, is important to meaningful communication. Be careful to avoid talking with a child just at times of crisis. This only teaches him that if he wants to have a serious

54

conversation, he'd better do something to upset you. Instead, spend time conversing with your children when things are pleasant and running smoothly. In this way you teach them that it's enjoyable to sit and talk with Mom and Dad. Often the best thing you can do to encourage your child to talk more is to be quiet yourself. If you can learn to keep your mouth shut and respond to what your children have to say, you'll usually find them becoming more comfortable talking to and around you.

Infant

Communication with an infant begins before mother and child are discharged from the hospital. A process called "bonding" or "attachment" takes place during the first month or so of life with a natural-born child, or during the first month after an infant is adopted. One way to greatly facilitate this attachment process is for *both* parents to learn caregiving skills as early as possible so both feel comfortable in their role as parents.

When parents are feeding, bathing, or diapering their infant,

they should be talking to her, playing with her, and, in general, just getting used to having a baby around. Feeding time presents an excellent opportunity to explore your infant, noting the fascinating detail in her fingers and toes, playing with her hair, and talking to her. The time a parent spends talking to an infant, provided you use normal words and not baby talk, is well spent, really an investment in the future because of the role this modeling plays in a child's later language development.

Toddler

Communication with a toddler is challenging because the toddler's language skills make it difficult for her to carry on a fluent conversation. Don't be fooled by this. Young children understand more complex language than they are able to produce. A toddler may be able to "read" only very simple books at first, in which she pairs single words like *tree, car,* and *dog* with the appropriate pictures, but she can understand you when you read classical childhood fairy tales or other simple stories to her.

The attention span of the toddler is frequently a source of concern to parents, simply because they expect too much. If you're going to read a story to your toddler, don't worry about whether you finish a page before you turn it or finish the book before you close it. The most important rule is to stop reading to your toddler before she gets bored or restless. This may mean that you start by reading to her for one minute or less. Do this daily for one or two weeks, perhaps several times a day, and you'll find that you can read to her for five minutes, then ten minutes. Pretty soon you'll have to set a limit on reading.

Children quickly learn to use bedtime stories as a way of getting to stay up late. You're the adult in your house—you make up the rules. Tonya gets a story at bedtime only if she's ready for bed on time. You may have to help her get ready, but if she fusses too much, skip the story. Set your portable timer for whatever time that you think is reasonable and that your child can tolerate. Tell her that you will read whatever story she wants you to read, and that when the bell on the timer rings, story time is over. Then, when the bell rings, give her a kiss (or whatever you choose to do at bedtime), tell her goodnight, turn off the light, leave the room, and close the door.

Preschooler

By the time children reach toddler and preschool age, they are fascinated by what goes on around them. You should thus make many of your interactions very social. If you're going for a ride in the car, converse with your child and point out things along the highway. If you're eating dinner at home or in a restaurant, talk with your child about what happened during the day, what's going to happen after dinner, and what will happen tomorrow. This helps the child's language development and begins teaching the concepts of yesterday, today, and tomorrow.

When it becomes part of your everyday life, neither you nor your child may be aware that teaching is going on. Although you may set aside times to read to your child and have your child read to you, incidental teaching at other times is as important as these more formal periods. Some television is educational. I recommend programs like "Sesame Street," particularly if a parent watches part of the program with the child and makes it a learning experience. For example, when letters are flashed on the screen, the parent can read them aloud to show the child (model for him) that it is appropriate to do so before the person on "Sesame Street" tells you what each letter is.

There are literally hundreds of situations in the normal course of a child's development that can be learning situations. Parents need to be alert, always watching for pleasant, natural situations that can be used in teaching.

School Age

Communication with a child follows a predictable pattern of development. Parents who communicate openly with their children and who encourage reasonable discussion, even about emotional issues, are often surprised by what they are able to discuss with their children. As an illustration, consider communication between parent and child about sex and related issues, such as dating. If parents recognize, from the beginning, the importance of communication about sexual matters, they will not avoid discussing other topics that may also make them a little uncomfortable.

With a younger child, questions about sex are fairly simple

(compared with what a teenager might ask), though they can make parents nervous. If, despite being a little nervous, you answer a child's question in as educated and sincere a manner as possible, she will recognize your openness and be encouraged to approach you again for further questions. You, in turn, will have survived an awkward but very important moment. Purposely giving out wrong information is asking for trouble later on. As parents begin to feel more comfortable talking about delicate issues, parents and children grow together.

Parents who choose not to discuss sex or related topics with a child until he reaches puberty may find that they can't handle the discussion when they are finally forced to face it. The child then has nowhere to turn except outside his home for answers. Children should be encouraged (by a receptive parental attitude) to discuss serious topics with either or both parents. As noted before, even though you gulp at the questions a preschooler or early school-age child may ask, these questions are nothing compared to those that will be in the child's mind when he or she is a teenager and begins dating.

Often, as a nervous response on the parent's part, a question asked by a child about sex will elicit a long and involved answer. The child usually doesn't want a lecture; he wants a discussion, and it takes two persons actively taking part to make a discussion. So, when your child (at whatever age) asks where babies come from, give her an accurate, relatively brief answer and then give her a chance to ask further questions. You may be surprised to find that she wasn't really asking what you thought. But, if you had gone off on some long-winded dissertation (or fantasy) about where babies come from, you would not have found out what she really wanted to know.

Remember, an older child is probably just as nervous about asking a sexual question as you are about answering it. She may have spent some time thinking about how best to pose the question so as to not offend you. However, in doing so, she may change her question so much that she doesn't get the answer she was looking for. A daughter asking a question about babies may be really asking about kissing or petting, but she doesn't feel comfortable enough to ask you about it directly. So, when your son or daughter asks a question about sex, try to remember that they're usually asking in the most tactful way they know. If you are receptive to their questions, then maybe the next time you talk about it, you'll get the real question.

Sex is only one of hundreds of topics that parents discuss with their children. The important thing to remember in any serious conversation is that your child is probably more nervous than you are. It's only through repeated conversations that you will both come to feel comfortable discussing important matters. It's a growth process. Understand and enjoy it for what it is.

Real Communication

Communication is one of the most important ways parents interact with their children, and children learn from the interaction. If communication is consistent and positive, it will be beneficial to the child. Lectures, threats, and warnings rarely bring about the changes intended by the parents. Communication, at its best, offers a constructive way to teach your child many of the things you want him to learn. If you are openly eager to share your knowledge with your child, and if you honestly seek to understand your child's needs (as well as his or her point of view), your child will come to see you as an understanding source of reliable information.

9

Modeling and Imitation

Children learn from what they see and hear you do. They learn more this way than by what you tell them. If they see you doing things around the house in a pleasant, matter-of-fact way, then that is how they tend to do things themselves. If, on the other hand, they see you always dissatisfied with what you have to do and hear you complain constantly, they'll realize that you're basically a pretty miserable person and they probably will make only limited efforts to get close to you. If your children see you and your spouse handle an argument in an emotional but rational way, and more importantly, if they see you resolve the argument, they will be a step closer to being able to do the same thing themselves. Each time your children see you and your spouse shouting at each other or maybe even throwing things, they will be one step closer to doing the same thing when they are grown.

Parents often wonder "Where did I go wrong?" because their children don't do well in school. The school may be blamed, sometimes rightfully. The important point is how often children see their parents engaging in the kind of behavior the school system expects. If a girl *never* sees her mom or dad reading anything at home, then chances are she will not develop an interest in reading. Very young children will climb into a chair with a book and sit and turn the pages if their parents read at home. When parents spend their evenings watching television, they shouldn't expect their daughter to go to her room and read. This doesn't mean that parents have to read every time their child has homework (although this makes the homework more enjoyable!). It does mean that children are more likely to learn to enjoy doing things they see their parents doing and enjoying.

Toddler

Many of the discussion points in the "Let Them Help You" chapter are relevant here. If a toddler sees his mother picking up his toys each day to straighten up the family room, and if she is relatively pleasant about doing it, then he will learn by imitation to pick up his toys. You can speed the whole process by giving love pats and encouragement when he makes even the slightest attempt at helping you, and seeing you do it sets an example he is likely to imitate.

There are many, many other things you can model for your toddler. Spending time playing with the baby and encouraging your toddler to do the same will help teach the toddler how you want the baby handled. In fact, parents many times find their children trying to model their parent's behavior before they are really ready to handle it. The example that comes to mind here is the five-year-old coming into the kitchen half carrying and half dragging his baby sister. He has seen his mother and father carrying the baby by picking her up under the arms, so now he's doing it, even though he's not tall enough or strong enough. The point is one that will come up again in the chapter on parents as teachers—what you do teaches your child what to do.

Preschooler

Most of the so-called educational toys on the market really aren't educational by themselves, but with the help of one or both parents toys can assist children in learning many things. Parents can spend time playing with their preschooler by coloring, putting puzzles together, and putting various-shaped blocks into their respective holes. As the child becomes more proficient at the individual game, the parent can gradually reduce the amount of time spent playing with the child and then continue with only verbal encouragement.

This is also a time when parents can be teaching social skills like "please" and "thank you" by modeling, as well as by noticing the child when she is doing these things. The mother can model things like sharing by inviting another child to play with one of her child's toys. Helping can be modeled by providing assistance to another family member while the preschooler is watching.

Parents can also model some thinking tasks for the preschooler.

You can hold up two jars and exaggerate your efforts to discern which is the heavier of the two. You might also encourage your pre-schooler to feel the weight of both jars and to try to decide which is heavier. Or, when pouring the contents of one container into another, you can encourage the preschooler to watch and ask him if he thinks all the liquid will fit into the new container.

School Age

By this time, a child's language development is usually suffi-ciently advanced for parents to begin more verbal modeling. You can prompt your child by asking comparative questions or questions about time and size. For example:

"Which of these (two things) is bigger?"
"Which of these is heavier?"
"How many pieces of gum do I have in my hand?"

"Sesame Street" does an excellent job in providing models for children's language development. Parents should take the time, oc-casionally, to watch this program with their child and to make an ef-fort to practice things they see. You can, for example, count houses, street lights, or people. You don't have to count very high, just count with your child, over and over and over again. Show her you are interested in what she is learning.

Parents can also model behaviors like saying nice things about persons who aren't present (as opposed to saying bad things about these same persons.) Parents of a school-age child really have an awesome modeling responsibility because school-age children are so very observant. They notice how Mom and Dad get along, how you treat other adults as well as other children, how you behave when you're happy and when you're upset. There's really no hiding from your child. Parents need to be constantly aware that they are setting daily examples that will very likely be followed.

Be a Good Model

Children learn by what they see and hear you do. All the lec-tures in the world will not compensate for the example that parents set for their children. If you are constantly smoking, drinking alco-hol, and running down your friends, associates, and even your chil-dren, you are showing your children that you expect the same behavior from them. If you are continually complaining about your spouse, or your house, or the fact that you don't have enough money to pay the bills, you are encouraging your child to do the same. This comes under the heading of what I call "sick talk"—complaining about all the misery and woe in your life. If you can't do anything about it, then why bring it up? And if you can do something about it, stop the "sick talk" and do something. Don't think that while you're sharing "sick talk" with a friend or relative over the telephone little Johnny won't learn it from listening. Unless you have a soundproof phone booth in your home, you can count on your children learning from your phone conversations.

"Sick talk" is one of the most damaging and destructive of all parent behaviors. Perhaps that's why I absolutely *hate* soap operas. They are almost always devoted to "sick talk," they are frequently bizarre, and viewers rarely learn anything from watching them. They're not even relaxing. No matter how you look at it, they are a waste of time. If you want to relax, tune in a nice, soft-music radio station and take a bath, or try reading a paperback best-seller instead—that will do you much more good than watching a "soapie."

10

Guidelines for Baby-sitters

Many mothers who don't work outside their homes say they don't want to leave their child with a baby-sitter because they don't think it is fair to the child. When a mother is spending twenty-four hours a day seven days a week with her child, she's not being fair if she doesn't occasionally line up a baby-sitter and get away. Parents need to find a good baby-sitter and day-care center and use them—not as an escape but as a breather.

In households with only one working spouse, if that parent spends a Saturday or a Sunday taking care of the children, he or she will find the homebound parent more pleasant and easier to get along with, and will also find out how much fun (and work) the children really are. Both parents need occasional times to be away from their children. These breathers can help make you more effective in your parenting job: away from the children, you broaden your own outlook and have time to consider the children and their development more objectively, without the almost constant pressure of some kind of care or instruction.

In selecting a baby-sitter, you should observe how the individual interacts with your child. Does the sitter look at the child and talk to her? Is the sitter warm and affectionate toward her? For example, if the child is standing next to the baby-sitter and talking to her, does the sitter put her hand on the child's back and look directly at him? Can the sitter discipline the child? Talk to the sitter specifically about this. Explain how you prefer to have your child disciplined, and try to get some idea of how the sitter will react when faced with having to do the disciplining.

There are several simple but often neglected or overlooked areas that need to be covered with a baby-sitter. Most parents will communicate to the sitter what they want the child to have for his next meal and where they'll be if the sitter needs to contact them, but you should also take time to write out the following information:

1. The parents' name, address, and phone number, and if the house is difficult to find, directions to it. This information should be in written form because in an emergency the sitter shouldn't have to rely on his or her memory.

2. The phone numbers of the local police and fire departments, and that of the family doctor.

3. The phone numbers of the electric and gas companies and the local water department.

4. The phone numbers of the neighbors closest to the family.

5. The phone numbers of next of kin in the event a crisis develops involving the parents.

6. The location of and directions for turning off the water supply to the house in the event a plumbing crisis develops.

7. The location of and directions for using the electrical fuse box.

8. The location of and directions for the fire extinguisher.

9. Instructions on how to answer the phone and your policy regarding visitors (I recommend that parents instruct sitters never to answer the door and certainly to admit no one).

If the parents are going to be gone for a couple of days at a time, perhaps a good distance from home, it is a good idea to have a lawyer draw up a "power of attorney" that allows the sitter (even if the grandparents are doing the sitting) to obtain medical care for the child should the need arise.

If the sitter has the preceding information, she or he will be able to act much more effectively if some emergency develops. It's best to go through the information, line by line, showing the sitter where the various things are and how they work. The extra time necessary to fully educate a sitter is insignificant compared to what it might help avoid in the event of an emergency.

In those families where both parents work and must leave the child with a baby-sitter for many hours each week, the choice and instruction of the baby-sitter is a significant responsibility. Remember that sitters are employees—they should be interviewed before they are hired. You should hire only an experienced sitter, and only after you have personally called his or her previous employers. Have the sitter come to your house (or you go to hers) for several hours so you can watch how she interacts with your children. Make it clear to your sitter that, on occasion, you will drop in to see how things are going without calling in advance. When you are paying someone to spend twenty to forty hours a week with your child, you have both the right and the responsibility to check on the sitter and inspect the way things are going.

You should spell out your ground rules before you hire a baby-sitter. If you have differences of opinion (such as in the use or application of discipline), discuss these in detail before you hire the sitter. And, if the sitter isn't working out, let him or her go! There's no sense in putting up with a sitter who's doing an inadequate job. Firing someone is unpleasant and difficult, but if the sitter's performance is inadequate and your children are getting poor care, you have a responsibility to get another sitter who can do the job.

Day-care centers should be chosen the same way—very carefully. Visit the center before enrolling your child. When you visit, concentrate on the interactions among the children and the workers. Don't give nearly as much weight to what they tell you they do as you do to what you *see* them do. Have a clear understanding that you can drop in, unexpectedly, to see how things are going. Feel free to discuss your feelings about how you want your child treated. If you can possibly avoid doing so, do not pay your child's tuition months or weeks in advance or sign a legally binding contract for six months or a year.

Infant

There are several things to look for when choosing a baby-sitter for your infant. Does the sitter seem genuinely interested in spending time with your child? There is considerable variability among sitters. Some like to just eat and watch television. Some make a conscious effort to interact with the children. Does the sitter handle your infant with confidence? This indicates experience with infants, which is more likely to be found in persons with infants of their own. Having an inexperienced teenager baby-sit with your infant for a couple of hours in the evening is all right, but if you have a sitter for forty hours a week, you need someone with experience. Experience is far more important than education. Very few persons learn anything about child rearing in school, so don't depend too much on education.

Toddler

The toddler age is a very active one for children. One minute they want to play with toys or games, the next minute they want to go outside for a walk. Make certain the sitter is willing to go outside to walk or supervise Hot Wheels riding or playing on the swing set. Look for imagination on the sitter's part. Most toddlers don't really care about the rules when they play a game, so it's best to have a sitter who's not a real stickler for this sort of thing. Toddlers need sitters with both patience and an ability to discipline without getting emotional.

Preschooler

Look for a sitter who is willing to talk with, read to, play with, and provide good pre-academic stimulation for your preschool child. At this age, children are more receptive to playing games according to the rules and they're more independent because they can ride bikes or tricycles (and are good at getting out of sight if not watched closely).

School Age

With a school-age child, the sitter may need to supervise homework (if you're lucky enough to live in a school district that still believes in homework). This requires some academic knowledge and an ability to give encouragement without nagging.

School-age children are also quite likely to want to have friends over, so you'll need a sitter who can stay on top of a situation without being too noisy or domineering.

Options for Older Children

I always used to wonder what parents did for baby-sitters when their children got to be nine to fifteen years old. The answer is now obvious to me. Instead of getting a baby-sitter, parents just farm their children out. One weekend my daughter has a friend overnight (which means that the friend's parents have one less child that night) and another weekend my daughter stays at a friend's house (which means that we have one less child that night). If the overnights are reasonably well balanced between your house and their house, you end up with a form of a co-op. Every couple of weeks things usually work out just right and you don't have any of your children at home. On those occasions, you and your spouse or friend can enjoy an evening out on the town or a quiet evening at home.

There are some obvious rules that you should consider adopting before you begin to use overnights in lieu of baby-sitters. One, don't let your child stay at another child's house until the other child has spent at least one or two overnights at your house and you've seen him in a variety of situations. In arranging the overnights you should get some opportunity to talk to the other child's parents. Try to make certain that they feel as strongly about supervision as you do.

Two, avoid situations where your child would be staying at a friend's home when his parents go out for the evening.

Three, whenever another child spends the night at your house, monitor the children quite often. Although you do not have to say that much, you want both your child and the other child to know that you keep a close eye on children in your home.

Four, try to plan activities with your child for overnights; whether it's games or videotapes, pizza or a movie, have some idea ahead of time what the children will be doing.

Five, always find out how to contact the other child's parents in the event of any emergency. You don't ever want to be left in the position of needing to leave the city because of a family emergency but not being able to because you have another family's child staying with you.

Six, do not allow children to spend another night in your home if the last time was a disaster. You should certainly make every attempt to discipline another child, but, when reasonable attempts fail, your only recourse is to contact the child's parents to let them know that you are unable to control their child. Though you may end up with some hurt feelings, this won't happen much, and overnights can be a nice screening tool for identifying children that you would just as soon not have your child playing with anyway.

Responsibilities

Baby-sitters are hired to interact with, supervise, and help or guide your children. Remember, they are in your employ as baby-sitters—if you want someone to do your laundry and dishes, you'll have to compromise on child care, which isn't advisable. Don't expect sitters to do any more than clean up whatever messes they make (wash their dishes, clean ashtrays they use, etc.). Also, try never to ask sitters to run your errands for you. It's not their responsibility to go to the grocery store for you or to pick up dry cleaning.

If you want a sitter who will take your children on short trips to the store or to the library, spell this out clearly before you hire him or her. Don't just pop up one day and say that you'd like the sitter to take the kids to the library.

Using relatives as sitters (sisters, grandmothers) usually means one thing—you're getting them for less than you'd have to pay a professional sitter. If the performance of a relative, as a sitter, is less than adequate, you owe it to your children to get another sitter.

Baby-sitting co-ops where mothers rotate taking care of each other's children are fine, providing that *each* of the other mothers does an adequate job and that the number of children doesn't get unwieldy. Large co-ops are trouble—no one person can adequately supervise eight or ten young children. Also, you may find that setting up a co-op with a good friend can strain the friendship. Put some thought into it before you get into a co-op that may be difficult to get out of gracefully.

Car pools are a form of a baby-sitting co-op. However, car pools require much more careful consideration because automobiles can be so dangerous to young children. Driving a car is difficult enough when you're alone, but if you have a car full of six or seven screaming, roughhousing kids, the job is even more difficult. If you are going to get into a baby-sitting co-op or a car pool, contact your insurance agent first. Insurance brokers are like lawyers in that they should be contacted *before* you go into a new venture, not *after* something has gone haywire.

Working Mothers

Now that over 60 percent of women in the U.S. work outside of their homes, many parents wonder what effect, if any, this has on the children from these homes. Some of the most frequently asked questions and their answers follow:

1. *Is it harmful for a mother to work outside the home?* This depends to a great extent upon the child-care arrangements the parent(s) make as well as how pleased the mother is to be working in the first place. There are no good research studies that document the effects

on children of alternative child-care arrangements. Nor are there any studies that have carefully compared child's-home day-care with out-of-child's-home day-care, with commercial day-care. There have certainly been some sensational cases where large numbers of children have been harmed in day-care, but fortunately these cases represent an almost infinitesimal percentage of the total child-care situation.

2. *How can you evaluate a substitute caregiving situation?* Talk with the caregiver that will be assigned to your child. Find out how his or her attitudes and practices compare with yours. The more time your child spends in alternate child-care, the more important it is for the alternate provider to have outlooks and viewpoints similar to yours. From a practical standpoint, look for a ratio of one adult to three infants less than two years of age, with the ratio increasing to one to four or one to five for older children.

3. *What are some of the possible negative effects on a child from the mother's working?* Inadequate caregiving is the major concern. Lack of supervision (as with latchkey children) may be another problem.

4. *When is it all right to return to work after the birth of a baby?* This decision should be based, at least in part, on the mother's physical health, the family's financial conditions, the mother-child relationship, the stability of the family, and the availability of adequate alternate child-care.

5. *What kinds of reactions can parents expect in themselves and their family if the mother returns to work with alternate day-care?* This depends a great deal on how satisfactory you find your alternate day-care arrangements. If they are expensive, difficult to get to, or less than what you really wanted, you can expect to be bothered until these deficiencies are corrected.

6. *Are there any special things mothers should keep in mind before they go back to work?* Mothers need a clear understanding with other family members about both child-care arrangements and responsibility for household duties. Generally, like a lot of other things, the planning and preparation that goes into alternate day-care arrangements will be reflected in the mother's satisfaction with the care that her child receives. The mother who works when she would rather be at home or the mother who stays at home when she'd rather resume her career are both going to be less than satisfied with alternate day-care. With adequate planning, support from family members, and a

true concern for what the mother wants, whatever trauma is involved in finding and utilizing day-care can be minimized.

What about Latchkey Children?

In recent times there is probably no child-related situation that we know less about but that has a greater potential for problems than latchkey child-care. Typically children in this situation are left for relatively short periods of time when they are young. A seven- or eight-year-old may be alone for only thirty minutes between when he gets home from school and when a parent returns to the home. At this age, it is unlikely that children will get into any remarkable situations, partially because of their age and naivete, and partially because they are intimidated by even venturing outside of their home. Over a period of months or even a year or two, the parents get a false sense of security because their child "handles" the latchkey situation so well.

By the time a child is thirteen or fourteen years old and problems become much more likely, it is difficult, if not impossible, for the parents to make alternate child-care arrangements—most in-home sitters would not stay with a child that age, particularly if the child were determined to get the sitter out. There are few commercial child-care agencies that will take teenagers. The rules that worked with a seven-year-old (no one else is allowed in the house or apartment and the child is responsible for completing chores after school) are difficult if not impossible to enforce when violated by a teenager.

Perhaps the most compelling argument against latchkey children is that no argument has ever been made that a child benefits from the latchkey arrangement. There is also little theoretical benefit for the latchkey child. Simply put, the latchkey arrangement saves parents the cost of adequate supervision at the risk of a child's health and welfare.

11

Divorce

Perhaps one of the most devastating things that can happen to a couple with children is to get a divorce. Try as many couples will, some just cannot make a go of their marriages. When this happens, there are always questions about how the divorce is going to affect the children. You as parents can minimize any bad effects that your children might feel. Divorce isn't necessarily damaging to children; rather, how parents handle the divorce and the issues surrounding it seems to make a big difference in how the children are affected. Perhaps the most significant issue is how much conflict there is between the parents.

Conflict

Children suffer the most when their parents are in constant conflict with one another. Parents who stay together and engage in constant conflict will see their children adversely affected, as will parents who get divorced and maintain a lot of conflict.

The point here is that it is the conflict, rather than the parents' marital status, that produces some of the adverse effects on the children of divorced couples. One effective way to minimize the conflict is for parents to arrive at a written agreement regarding custody, times of changes, places of changes, etc., and then stick to that agreement as much as humanly possible. If Dad is supposed to pick the children up at 6:00 p.m. at Mom's house, then he should be there at 6:00 to pick them up and they should be ready to be picked up. Generally, pick-up and drop-off times should be kept as short as possible, literally completed within a minute or two. I recommend that Dad not come into the house and socialize with Mom. Mom's social life and Dad's social life are no longer the other parent's business. Also, the less you know about what your ex is doing, the less judgmental you are going to be.

Modeling

If you handle your divorce and the custody changes matter-of-factly and unemotionally, your children are more likely to do the same. On the other hand, if you get kind of "crazy" every time custody changes, your children are more likely to follow your example.

It is very important that you remain either neutral or positive about your child's other parent. Try hard never to put him or her down in front of your children or, for that matter, in front of other people. A divorce should not only separate the parents from each other, it should also separate their concerns for each other. This is often easier said than done. So many times parents will make comments about their ex that are negative or even ugly, then justify the comment by saying something like, "You just don't know how mean your Dad was to me." There's no excuse for making such statements to a child about their own parents, so try to refrain from doing so as much as possible.

An issue closely related to modeling is what kind of a relationship you have with your child after a divorce. If you and your ex always wanted your children to sleep in their own rooms, then keep that up after the divorce. I can't count the number of times I've heard parents say that they were sleeping with their child as a source of comfort to the child. Generally, parents who sleep with a child after a divorce are doing it to comfort *themselves,* not the child. They just use the excuse of wanting to comfort the child to cover up their own feelings. Try to behave as much like you did before the divorce as you can.

Another related issue concerns discussing the divorce with your children. Typically such discussions are for the parent, not for the child. Find another adult or find a therapist, but don't use your own child as a sounding board. Sure, it's difficult after you've been hurt by a divorce, but you won't help anybody by confiding in your children the worries or concerns that you have about the divorce.

Spying

Don't ask your child for information about what is going on at the other parent's house—not out of concern for your children, not out of idle curiosity, and not out of pure nosiness. After a separation and divorce, it is, to put it bluntly, none of your business what your ex is doing. You can say that you are just looking out for your children, but in reality most of these kinds of questions have little potential for any positive outcome and great potential for harm.

Social Life

Generally speaking, it's none of your concern what your ex does with his or her own time or the time spent with the children. If you could change your ex, then you would probably still be married. Living apart after a divorce, there is really nothing you can do to change your ex, but there seems to be a lot of harm that you can do your children. Your best bet is to stay out of each other's lives as much as possible.

Visitation

As hard as it may be to believe, the actual visitation schedule does not seem to affect the children. Whether a child is with one parent one or two weekends a month, two weeks in a row every month, or a couple of days every week, how the parents handle the visitation and any changes that arise is more important than the schedule itself.

Money

Most children don't know much about finances and therefore shouldn't be either consulted or used in an effort to gain an economic advantage over the other parent. You have no business telling your children that you would like to take them someplace but can't, because your ex-wife gets most of your paycheck or because your ex-husband doesn't pay you enough to live on. There's a temptation, of course, to blame your ex, a perfectly understandable one; just don't drag your children right into the middle of it. It may be a good idea to arrange, at the time of the divorce, to have all financial payments go to the court, not to your ex; that way, late payments are handled by the court.

Divorce, unfortunately, is a part of life for many people. While the divorce always has a negative impact on the parents who get divorced, there are a number of things that you can do or not do that can minimize the effects of the divorce on your children. The handout on divorce at the end of this book, written by Dr. Nicholas Long, has some good suggestions for couples who have gotten a divorce and who want to do what's best for their children. Although some of these suggestions may be hard to follow, they are almost all easier than correcting a child's emotional problems, once established.

12

Automobile Travel

Traveling by auto brings concerns about both the safety and the behavior of children in transit. Much has been written about the safety aspects of infant and child car seats, and the evidence favoring safety restraints is overwhelming. Virtually all physicians now recommend that the baby's first trip in a car, the trip home from the hospital, be made in a tested and approved infant safety seat. If you don't already have one of these, read an objective report on child restraint seats (perhaps the best is the study done by and reported in *Consumer Reports,* which is updated every few years), then purchase a safety seat and use it each time you take your child out in the car.

A research study on safety restraint seats sponsored by General Motors (Love Seat Division) noted that children behave much better on auto trips if they are in a safety seat. They are much less likely to stand up, hang out of a window, or climb all over the driver. (It's a little difficult to jump around when you're strapped down!) There are times when children will be very unhappy in a car seat, but don't give in to this unhappiness. The child's life may very well depend on using an adequate car seat. Once you have taught your child to ride this way, your trips will be more enjoyable and much safer. You might even try wearing a seat belt yourself (modeling). Other advantages of restraint seat usage include less car sickness (in toddlers), fewer distractions to the driver, better sleeping on long rides, and less concern for injuries that might occur during regular auto travel.

If you haven't been using a car seat, your child will almost certainly express a great deal of unhappiness when you begin. You can expect the first six to ten trips to be a minor war between your child and the car seat. If you stick to your decision to use the car seat and catch your child being good in it at every opportunity, you'll find that he soon adapts to riding in one.

It is important how you interact with your child during auto trips. Parents typically fall into the trap of talking about things that are of interest to them but which bore children. Some of the conversation should include the children. To minimize boredom on long trips, many parents invent games to keep both themselves and their children occupied. For example, with toddlers you can point out when you are going under a bridge by getting the child's attention, pointing to the bridge as you approach it, and saying "Here we go, under the bridge" (drag out the word *under* until after you've passed under the bridge). "See, we went under the bridge." You can do this, too, when you pass a truck or a truck passes you.

Look for anything that is the least bit unique to engage your child's attention—cows or boats or airplanes. The important thing is to show an interest in what your child is learning. With preschool-age children, if you've been in touch with the school, you can find out what things your daughter's teacher is covering and include these in your automobile conversation. By carrying on pleasant interactions with your children during car rides, you make the whole trip more pleasant while improving your child's language skills.

If you are having problems with your child during short daily trips in the car, try a series of brief "training trips." First, when the trip involves just one adult and one child, place the child's restraint seat in the front passenger seat (not the back)—it's much easier to interact with a child you can see and touch. Avoid the temptation to ignore your child until he has done something that annoys or irritates you—start by giving your child feedback right away when he's sitting quietly. Suggest that he look at various things, pointing out objects that might be of interest. Make sure these trips are very short at first. Gradually lengthen them as your child's behavior in the car improves. These training trips teach behaviors that make subsequent car trips much more pleasant.

Infant

Pregnant women should wear a seat belt and shoulder belt (if available) throughout the entire pregnancy. Every infant traveling in an automobile *belongs* in an infant car carrier. There is no safe alternative. The most dangerous place in a car for an infant is in her mother's arms. If you have an infant, or are expecting one (yourself or through adoption), buy an infant car carrier and use it. These infant carriers are good from birth until your baby weighs eighteen to twenty pounds. Follow the manufacturer's instructions very carefully and switch to a toddler seat as soon as the instructions supplied with the infant seat tell you to do so.

Toddler and Preschooler

Most toddler car seats are designed for children who weigh twenty to forty pounds. Get an approved car seat and use it *every time* you go out in the car. Many toddlers become so accustomed to riding there that they remind their parents to put them in the car seat.

As mentioned earlier, traveling time is a good time to converse with your child and point out things of interest along the roadside. This helps occupy his time and keeps his mind off the fact that he is in the car seat. When your child gets old enough to count, you can practice counting street lights, houses, or whatever. Children enjoy this attention and it gives parents opportunities for teaching things about the outside world.

School Age

After your child weighs approximately forty pounds, it's time to switch from a toddler safety seat to a booster seat with the auto seat belt. Booster seats are much easier to use and work until a child is eight to ten years old. Use only the seat belt—*do not* use the shoulder belt until the child is above the height specified by the car manufacturer. One reason children stand up in a car is because they can't see out. If you place them in a booster seat and then put on the seat belt, they'll be able to see outside and still travel safely. You can stop using the booster seat when your child can sit in the regular car seat, with the seat belt on, and be able to see out of the window.

Always Use Car Seats

Children learn how to behave in the car by riding in the car with you. If you consistently use an age-appropriate car seat, then your child will behave very well while riding and will be safer in the event of a sudden stop, turn, or accident. If you do not use a car seat, you will probably end up nagging your child about sitting down, about fighting with brothers or sisters, or more serious things like hanging out a window. Make your life easier—buy and use child car seats.

When parents tell me that their child was banned from a car pool because he wouldn't behave in someone else's car, they've overlooked a simple answer: car seats. If your children are in a car pool, put in the extra effort required to get the other drivers to use the car seat, at least for your child. It may mean life or death.

13

Shopping and Other Excursions

Each time you go into a supermarket or eat at a restaurant that caters to young families, you see some children who behave very nicely and some who behave very poorly. This difference reflects their training. Community settings can be trouble spots for two reasons. One, parents are easily distracted from their primary role as teachers, and two, parents frequently relax their rules when they're out in a community setting.

The shopping center presents a unique learning situation for children whose parents view a trip to the store in this fashion. The grocery store offers literally hundreds of opportunities for children to learn about numbers, shapes, textures, weights, and sizes. But in order to take advantage of these opportunities, the parents have to see the store for what it is: a teaching situation. As described in the chapter on modeling and imitation, your children are learning when they are with you. If you go into the grocery store and ignore your child until she does something wrong (catch 'em being bad?), you set yourself up for future unpleasant shopping trips by teaching the child to get attention through misbehavior.

Going to the grocery store can test your working knowledge of the guidelines discussed so far. You must monitor your children closely to catch them when they're being good, you should let them help you, and you have to be prepared to discipline them when necessary. For a toddler, the only discipline necessary is to ignore a temper tantrum. For example, it is very common for a toddler to reach out and grasp a candy bar while you are unloading the shopping cart at the checkout stand. If you take the candy bar away, say "No!", and then do not give in to the resulting screaming (even though you are terribly embarrassed!), you will teach your daughter that she cannot take candy bars while in the checkout line. However, if you let her keep it or give it back to her when she starts screaming, then you are teaching her to do the same thing next time she has the opportunity. One thing that makes the grocery store a difficult territory is the tempting way the stores display products. (It sometimes appears that someone who likes to cause trouble between parents and children designed the displays.) There's little you can do to change the store—your only choice is to teach your child how to behave there.

These same guidelines apply when you take your child to a restaurant, where you're tempted to discuss things with your spouse, you have a tendency to ignore the children, and you tend to relax the rules a little. Fortunately, restaurant behavior is easy to practice at home. It isn't necessary at every meal, but you should have some meals at home when the children dress up and practice their best manners. For many children, if the parents do it right, this is an enjoyable and festive occasion. During these special meals, parents should concentrate on exactly how each child is behaving and give feedback about behavior. This means that parents must model what they consider to be appropriate behavior, and they should catch 'em being good. These special meals are meant to concentrate entirely on how the children are behaving, for the sole purpose of teaching them how you want them to behave in a restaurant. Once you've taught your children how to behave during dinner at home, you will also feel free to invite guests to your house for dinner without being embarrassed.

If you are faced with having to discipline your child while in a restaurant or other public place, you have several options other than those mentioned in the preceding section on grocery stores. In clothing stores, at the swimming pool, or at the park, you can tell a child who misbehaves to sit quietly at a particular spot for a minute or two. In the park, for example, you can tell him to sit on the park bench next to where the entire family is eating. At the pool, make him sit on a chair or bench away from the water, but where he can still see the other children having a good time. The length of time is not really as important as the fact that your son knows you *are* going to enforce the rules when you're away from home. There are times when you may have no choice but to take him out to the car for a couple of minutes until he gets calmed down. Don't worry about what the other people are thinking—just concentrate on getting your child's behavior under control while he's still young enough to handle. If you think it's embarrassing to have a two-year-old act up in a restaurant, think what it's like to get the same thing from a ten- or twelve-year-old.

Infant

Infants should be taken both to grocery stores and to restaurants. At first they just ride along in their infant seats, but even this gives you an opportunity to make the trip a pleasant experience by touching and talking to them. These trips also serve to get the infant adjusted to being around crowds and noise and motion. You can periodically lean over to your infant and touch him gently to "catch him being good," even though he isn't capable of behaving any other way. You will be wise to start your infant off knowing that trips to stores and restaurants are fun because Mom and Dad pay a lot of attention to him.

Toddler

At this age you still have the advantage of being able to put your child in either the shopping cart or in a high chair at a restaurant. (You can use a folding canvas stroller for department stores.) Then you have to watch him closely enough to be able to give him lots of feedback about how he's doing.

People who design grocery store displays place all the candy and gum out where you wait in line at the cash register. This is so tempting to toddlers that every parent has fallen prey to it at some time or another. As discussed previously, if your toddler reaches out and picks up a candy bar, she will probably give some indication that she's unhappy if you try to take it away. Be careful. If you immediately give the candy bar back to her, then you just taught her that if she wants a candy bar, all she has to do is reach for it and then fuss if you try to take it away.

What you should do in this situation is 1) provide a lot of brief, nonverbal, physical contact whenever you're in a checkout line and your child doesn't touch anything, and 2) if she does pick up something, take it away immediately and put it back on the shelf. Let her fuss all she wants, but don't return the candy bar. If the person at the

cash register says anything, just reply that your daughter is learning to leave store things alone.

Preschooler

The preschool age is when most parents, if they're going to have trouble with their children in public places, start having it. Preschoolers get around so well that it is easy for them to get away from their parents and race off through a store. Most parents report at least minor problems with their children in settings like the grocery store. A solution is for one parent to start making short training trips to the store, maybe fifteen minutes in length. These fifteen minutes should be spent actually working with the child on how to behave in the store.

Start off, upon entering the store, by telling your child to stay with you, then praise her for staying with you before she has a chance to get away. This praise should occur every fifteen or twenty feet at first and then gradually reduced to the end of each aisle. You should also offer your child praise and attention for not handling items on the store shelves. In the training trip, the parent's attention should be on the behavior of the child—it really doesn't make any difference whether you buy anything on the first trip or two. Parents should plan the length of the training trip so they're ready to leave the store before the child has misbehaved.

Our studies have shown that the flavor of these training trips should always be as positive as possible. If the child strays from the parent or touches items that the parent says are off limits, one thing that will frequently work is placing the preschooler in the shopping cart for one minute, with a very brief explanation such as "Stay with me." The least effective thing you can do is to warn your child the first time he wanders away from the cart. The *first* time the rule is broken is the time the child should be very matter-of-factly placed in the cart with a brief explanation (no more than four words) of why he is there. One minute later (if he is quiet), take him out of the cart, place him on the floor next to you, and say, "Stay close to me." (If the child is screaming, leave him in the cart until he is quiet for fifteen seconds.)

A point made in the introduction is well made again here—this book is written primarily for parents who are having only *minor* problems with their children. It's impossible, of course, to pick examples that are relevant to each and every parent, and the examples offered here are taken from situations most frequently encountered in my practice. Using the example of a child not staying with his parents in the store doesn't mean that all children *should* stay with their parents in the store. This is a decision that parents must make. If you want your child to stay with you, then you should use the procedures described.

There may be other behaviors not covered here that are important to you. If so, use the same general idea of training trips to teach your son or daughter how you want them to behave. This book recommends and describes procedures that will work for you, but you must decide what behaviors you want to develop in your child. If you aren't having problems in the grocery store, then you can use the principles of monitoring and "catch 'em being good" to teach your child other things in the store.

School Age

Most parents do not have serious problems with their children in community settings, but if you are and the children are school age or above, you should ask your family doctor to recommend someone who can help you to work on those problems. The procedures described for preschoolers will work with school-age children as long as you have control over them. If you can't get your children to mind you at all, then I suggest you work on that problem at home before you begin to worry about behavior in the grocery store.

Community Settings

The point must be clear now that children learn how to behave in community settings by what their parents teach them. If you are having problems in any community setting—grocery stores, restaurants, church or synagogue—you need to take the basic principles outlined and adapt them to your particular situation. You should schedule training trips to the problem setting. In the case of improper church behavior, until corrected at least one parent will have to go to services knowing that he or she will be there for only ten or fifteen minutes and that the purpose of the trip is to teach the child how to behave appropriately during services. In the interim, this parent has to temporarily give up whatever gratification comes from going to church. In many situations (like church services or ceremonies), it is unrealistic to expect a small child to remain attentive the whole time. That's why many public gathering places now have a nursery, so parents can participate in the activity that's drawn them there without worrying about noise from their children. Expecting children to behave for long periods when they are young, in situations like churches and theaters, is unreasonable. Better to get a good baby-sitter and let the parents enjoy the activity without expecting too much from the children.

On the other hand, don't use a baby-sitter for years while you go to church and then suddenly expect a seven-year-old to be able to sit through an hour-long service. Whenever you decide to teach your child how to behave in church, you should start with brief trips there. Over a period of weeks and months, gradually lengthen the amount of time you spend in church. The way you know you've lengthened the time too soon is if your child starts acting up every time. At that point you should go back to shorter trips so that your child learns that you leave church while she's still behaving. Whatever you do, don't wait for her to misbehave each time before you leave. That's catching her being bad. Also, it's unfair to others to stay through an entire service while you're nagging your child to "be quiet" or "stop that" or "sit still."

Community settings are pleasant places to take your children if you keep in mind that they're learning the whole time they're there, and you are the one most responsible for what they learn.

14

Toys

Parents must respond to children's needs for something to play with, which entails selecting from an unrelenting barrage of gadgets and advertising claims that every toy is not only irresistible but educational too! You need live with a child only a short time to find out that many toys are not irresistible and that few toys, by themselves, are really educational. Many toys can be educational when used appropriately by the parent and the child, but if the parent is resourceful, the same teaching can usually be done with makeshift toys or ones less expensive than the so-called "educational" toys.

Toys are intended to occupy children so that you don't have to spend all your time with them, and so that your child will begin to learn isolate play skills. Children learn through exploring, manipulating, seeing things move, and hearing things make different noises. If a child is to be kept occupied for reasonable lengths of time, and if he is to learn anything from this occupation, then he needs toys that hold his attention. The most important consideration in selecting a toy is whether the child will play with it more than once, and whether he will play with it for more than one or two minutes at a time. Every parent has brought home an appealing toy only to find that the child couldn't care less about it. Toy manufacturers, the federal government, and consumer testing groups should be testing toys constantly and reporting which toys maintain attention. Unfortunately, there are few if any published reports saying which toys, or types of toys, attract and hold a child's attention. What then can parents use as a basis for decision, at least until evaluations of toys are available?

The best guess about what toys a child will play with consistently can be made by noting what toys you have seen your child play with in the past. (I say "guess" to leave room for that fickleness of children that we've all come to appreciate over the years.) If you are at a friend's house and your child plays with the same toy each time you go there, then chances are he'll play with the same toy at home. If your daughter loves to ride on a neighbor's Big Wheel, then buying one for her would be a good investment.

In one study we found that some toys are used only in a group situation (that is, when there is more than one child playing) and some are usually played with only when a child is alone. So, if you have an only child, and you find that he loves to play catch with his friends, buying him a ball will occupy his time only when he is with his friends. When choosing a toy, keep in mind the play circumstances you expect for your child. Examples of social toys include checkers, chess, and other board games, as well as balls and other sports items. Some isolate or individual toys are crayons, Tinkertoys, Lego, and Play Doh.

Parents can sometimes prompt a child to play alone with a toy by first playing with it together. This doesn't always work, but it is a good way to tell whether you can expect your child to learn to play with the toy himself. Try demonstrating the toy, but don't concern yourself with how it should "best" be used. Children frequently use toys in ways parents never dreamed of. A good example would be giving a Monopoly game to a younger child. Chances are he'll put the pieces that move into his mouth, and he may chew on or throw around the "Chance" cards. You can be sure only that he isn't going to set out all the play money and begin a correct game of Monopoly, particularly if he's by himself.

When you start playing with a toy with your child, be sure to make the experience as pleasant as possible (catch 'em being good). You defeat the purpose of a toy (occupying a child's time) if you get angry and shout at a child because he isn't using a toy correctly. The one exception to this concerns safety—some emotion is natural when your child is endangering himself. Most of the time, though, when parents become emotional or angered by the way a child uses a toy, it's not because what she's doing is unsafe—it's because she isn't using the toy the way the parent thinks it should be used. This sort of reaction certainly won't nourish the child's interest in playing with the toy later.

Another general rule is to try to limit (on any given occasion) the number of toys a child has to select from. In some homes you can barely walk through the sea of toys. Children don't have time to play even momentarily with dozens of toys in a typical period of play.

Parents should limit the number of toys available at one time by storing extra toys in some inaccessible place. You can then rotate them, always keeping the ones your child plays with and storing those he doesn't play with. Eventually you'll have a small collection of toys your child favors.

Toys also provide a means for parents to begin socializing their children. Children can be taught to share, if you want them to learn how to share, by being encouraged to let another child borrow a toy. Your child may be very reluctant at first to let another child have one of his toys, but after finding out how pleased you are about his sharing and going to time-out a couple of times for refusing to share, he may encourage a friend to take one.

Infant

A mobile over the crib is the first toy many children encounter. Child development experts approve of mobiles because they offer moving visual stimulation, some provide music, and all react to the baby's touch. Mobiles are frequently used to occupy a baby between the time of waking and the time when one of her parents comes for the next feeding (we hope before the baby starts to cry!).

Several commonsense rules apply to the selection of toys for infants. Do not overburden a child with too many different toys in the crib. If your baby has thirty different toys, rotate them occasionally, leaving the toys the baby plays with the most and adding one or two other ones. Remember that your baby has to *sleep* in the crib too, so try to keep the number of toys down to three, four, or five.

Picking safe toys for babies is extremely difficult because no toy manufacturer admits that his toy is unsafe and very little research has been done on toy safety. So, start with the obvious dangers. Stay away from toys with lead paint on them, those with sharp points, those with small pieces that might be swallowed or inhaled (such as the cute eyes on some dolls or stuffed animals), or those that have plastic beads inside them. Damaged bean bags should either be repaired or thrown out *immediately,* since infants and children can easily inhale the small beans.

Most infants really enjoy a wind-up swing that comes with its own stand or that hangs in a doorway. Some children will sit contentedly in one of these for as long as it's swinging, and some quickly fall asleep.

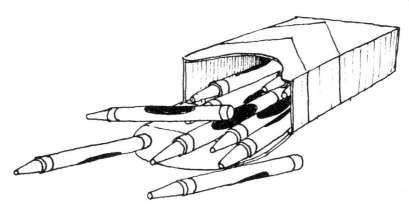

Toddler and Preschooler

The toys that toddlers and young children are most likely to play with are construction toys, such as colored blocks and Lincoln Logs; creative-artistic toys, such as crayons, Play Doh, soap bubbles, and watercolors; and mobile toys, which can be ridden or pulled. In selecting toys, consider some research findings we identified in our research:

- There was no correlation between cost and use; low-cost items such as crayons and bubbles fared very well.
- Age recommendations given by the manufacturers were unreliable; toys marked for older children were found to be as popular with younger children and vice versa. Most age estimates are just guesses.
- The sex of a child is as important as age in toy appeal; girls preferred artistic toys while boys preferred construction toys, although both kinds of toys were popular with the other sex as well.
- Some toys quickly attracted children but not for long. (Watch for this when you're in the store, because toys that are cleverly packaged to attract a child's attention are not necessarily toys children will play with.)
- Some toys look safe on the outside but when broken expose a variety of hazards.
- Some toys (games) naturally encourage social play (involving more than one child); examples of such were playing cards and fingerpaints.
- Some toys naturally encourage solo play; some noted were

Tinkertoys, crayons, Play Doh, and toys that make a sound or phrase with the pulling of a string.

Although we know of no research on outdoor toy use, children do enjoy riding toys and swinging toys. The best way to select outdoor toys is to observe your child at play at another child's house or at a local park or recreation center. If you observe him playing with the same toys on several occasions, there's a better than even chance that he'll play with it at home. (Provided you don't expect your child to use a social toy in solo play.)

School Age

The likes and dislikes of school-age children vary greatly. Some children enjoy music and books, some enjoy heavy physical sports (football), and some enjoy lighter sports (hiking, horseback riding). In addition to observing her with toys or sporting goods, it's a good idea to encourage your child to sample new activities. For example, you might go to a local recreation area and rent a small boat for an hour on several occasions. You may find that, after enough time has passed to begin to "get the feel of it," your child develops a preference for a new activity that you can also enjoy. Depending on where you live, the line of activities is almost limitless, from trips to the library to spectator and contact sports.

Sharing Toys

The selection of toys and activities by parents, and the use of them by children, can serve both immediate and long-term goals in

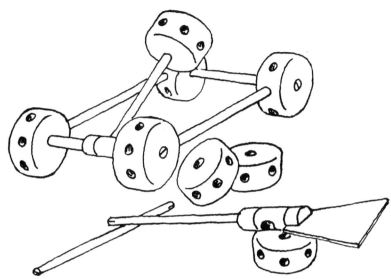

child development. With good adult supervision, toys may assist children in learning some very important, but very difficult concepts such as sharing. Children can learn the word "mine" in one day at preschool, but it may take them a year to learn the meaning of "sharing." Parents can encourage a child to learn to share by pointing out, briefly, that *they* are sharing each time they give him a drink of their iced tea or Coke. They can also foster such concepts by asking the child to share his Coke with them—children, like adults, would much rather share spinach than they would ice cream.

15

Parents Are Teachers

The point has been made repeatedly that parents are teachers. Whether or not you intend it, plan it, or *like* it, you teach your children by your everyday interactions with them. You son learns how to get attention by getting attention. He learns how to get along with others by watching you and by experimenting in getting along with other people. If helping his little sister gains your attention, then he'll do it to get attention. If mistreating his little sister is the only way to get your attention, then he'll do that in order to get your attention. All your speeches and lectures combined will not offset the influence of how you personally interact with your son.

Your reaction to your child's behavior when you are having an interesting telephone conversation presents an excellent example to further clarify this point. As long as your daughter behaves herself, you go right on talking. You wouldn't interrupt what you're doing for anything. Who ever heard of a parent saying "Just a minute, Barbie is playing nicely with her sister; I'll be right back"? But if your daughter starts teasing her little brother, for example, then you *immediately* say "Just a minute," put the phone down, and go see what's happening. As soon as the situation is under control, you return to your phone call.

In this example, what you're doing, though unwittingly, is teaching your daughter that if she wants to get you away from the phone, she'd better get into something because being good won't work. Parents don't sit down and think to themselves, "I'm going to talk on the phone until Barbie gets into trouble." But you get trapped into doing this when you aren't tuned into catching your child being good. It is possible to talk effectively on the phone for lengthy periods if you're willing to pause periodically and give your child some brief feedback on how he's doing. Without this feedback, children will start to harass you when you're on the phone, and when they do, it means you've waited too long to give them lots of love pats for behaving nicely while you're busy.

Too Much Feedback?

Many parents are reluctant to give their child intensive feedback because they fear he will grow up expecting feedback and often be disappointed. Nonsense. If you found out that your son's teacher never graded his classwork or homework, you'd wonder what kind of teacher he had. You can't teach without giving feedback.

In almost every educational setting, from the building and construction trades to medical school, the apprentice, student, or trainee is given intensive feedback while he is learning. In fact, when we want to teach people something complex we usually start off by having them watch someone who knows how to do whatever it is we're teaching. When they've watched it being done by an expert many times, then we let them try it with the expert watching and giving feedback at each step. Although there are enormous differences, of course, between teaching welding or scuba diving and teaching a child how to talk, or get along with other people, or to show good manners, the learner slowly gets better at doing whatever it is we're trying to teach, and sure enough, the student eventually becomes a teacher.

What better situation can you think of for teaching a child than to have him live with his teacher (you) for a long time (about twenty years) with continuous feedback? Certainly, as your child gets older you'll be teaching him different things. But from your earlier teachings, each new task will be a little easier. Parents are teachers for many years, and children are students of life while they live with you. Your job, whether you acknowledge it or not, is to teach them everything you know about how to survive, as pleasantly and equitably as possible.

There's a sense of satisfaction and inner accomplishment in teaching a child that can't be matched in any other situation. Being a parent may very well be the most difficult job on this earth and the one for which we are the least well prepared. But it's also the most rewarding job. There is absolutely nothing that compares to seeing a child take his first step or hearing him say "Mommy" or "Daddy" for the first time. Observing children come up with ideas that you never dreamed of and knowing that their minds are working a mile a minute is a mixture of fascination and wonderment that only a parent can appreciate.

We are wise to cultivate and cherish and provide all the opportunities we can to experience these good things that come free with being a good parent.

16

Television

Years ago, before the invention of television, parents gave their children pacifiers to keep them quiet. Now many parents just turn the television on, and the child just sits there watching whatever is on the channel the parents have selected. It doesn't matter whether it's a soap opera (of no practical use to either parent or child and probably detrimental to both), a cops-and-robbers shoot 'em up, a mindless game show, or whatever. Instead of walking through a park, window shopping, playing on a school playground, sitting together reading a story, or just talking with each other (any of which would benefit both parent and child and contribute to a pleasant interaction between them), they sit in front of the television set and do nothing.

The main problem with television is that parents do not use discretion in what they allow themselves or their children to watch. I see nothing wrong with a parent *and* child watching "Sesame Street." A parent can model saying the numbers and letters out loud for the child and very quickly notice the child starting to say them back. If "Sesame Street" has a program with a deaf or blind child, for example, this provides a suggestion and a stimulus for parents to discuss something significant with their child. After such a show, you can have your daughter hold her hands over her ears while you talk very softly to her. In this way she can gain some small appreciation of what it must be like to have a severe hearing loss.

There are numerous programs about wildlife and Walt Disney characters that are appropriate for children. However, about 90 percent of what's on television is not only *not* beneficial to a child, but may actually be detrimental. The best rule to follow is not to even turn the set on unless you want to watch a specific program that you have some reason to believe might benefit your child; then, having watched the program to its conclusion, shut the television off. As mentioned in the chapter on modeling and imitation, if you turn on the television set and watch whatever happens to come on, you are *teaching* your son or daughter to turn on the television set and watch whatever happens to come on. If, on the other hand, you only turn on the set when you have a specific show to watch and then you turn it off, you are *teaching* your son or daughter to watch only specific programs and to find other ways to occupy their spare time.

What kinds of programs do I recommend for children? Parents should choose programs that children can learn something from and those that provide healthy entertainment. Unfortunately, such programs only appear for an hour or two a day, so you'll have to work at filling the rest of the time.

What kinds of programs do I discourage?

Violent programs. Children certainly do not need to have violence modeled for them. Violent programs can and do teach children to be violent, which is something no reasonable parent would intentionally teach.

Soap operas. Why do so few experts speak seriously against soap operas? (Maybe the experts watch them.) The reason I don't recommend these programs for anyone, parents or children, is that although they depict life in a way that seems believable, any similarity between soap operas and real life is purely coincidental. Soap operas are frequently depressing to mothers and fathers, which does not help make them good parents. As unrealistic as they actually are, unfortunately soap operas resemble real life in a distorted but clever way; without thinking it can be difficult to discriminate between what happens on these shows and what happens in real life.

Game shows. Interestingly, almost every teenager I have worked with who had real problems in school preferred to stay home and watch soap operas and game shows. Why? Probably because they are fantasies and do not require much energy expenditure. Game shows present mindless trivia, depicting get-rich gimmicks that are beyond practically everyone who watches them.

Situation comedies. Like soap operas and game shows, situation comedies depict a life that doesn't exist, a fantasy that is at best misleading and completely devoid of intellectual stimulation.

If you and your children decide not to sit around and watch television, what are you going to do? You'll have to take an active part in your child's education and in his recreation, planning activities to fill the day. You'll have to actively spend time doing things with your children, like working around the house, going for walks, sitting and talking, and enjoying the members of your family.

The more difficult it is for you to give up television viewing, the more important it is for you to give it up. Television is an addiction, much like cigarette smoking. Many adults say "I can quit watching television any time I feel like it"; when you ask them why they don't quit, though, they say that they don't feel like it. Another common comment is "Oh, it's on, but I'm not really paying any attention to it." Fine, but if you shut if off be prepared to listen to screams of protest!

We live in a generation that was raised on television. It has been our constant companion for as long as most of us can remember. Like many other problem areas, television is easier to prevent than it is to cure. If you are expecting a child or have a small infant at home, don't watch television any more than four or five hours a week, and then only when programs have some social or educational value. If you can discipline yourself to keep the television set off, you'll find that your children are less likely to get hooked on it. Find interesting or constructive or relaxing things to occupy your time, activities that don't require you to sit in one spot and stare for hours on end at images of dubious value.

One absolutely sick scene that unfortunately is also quite prevalent finds the parents sitting in front of the television set, watching some popular, violent program and yelling at the kids to get into their rooms and do their homework. If you want your children to do their homework, set aside a time in the evening when you read quietly and expect your children to do the same. Then, after reading or homework is completed, discuss what the children read or did on their homework. You'll be surprised at how much you both learn. There's also nothing wrong with spending time in the evening sewing or working on the car or playing games with the children. You'll find that you never dreamed your children were as enjoyable as they are, and you'll also find that your children spend less time being disruptive.

All of the guidelines in the preceding chapters will be easier to implement if you watch television less. Television is a useful tool and can be very helpful when watched selectively. However, when watched indiscriminately and almost continuously, it can have a truly destructive influence on you and on your family life.

Common Behavior Problems

The discussion up to this point has introduced some general ideas to consider in living with and teaching your children. The focus of the sections that follow shifts to some of the specific problems that parents most commonly encounter with their children at various ages. If you've read and understood the chapters up to this point, then the groundwork is there for the following discussions to be very helpful. If you've skipped the preceding text, though, and are ready to jump right into the problems, there's good chance that you'll never get it right.

If your child is experiencing difficulties at mealtime, bedtime, or with toilet training, you should concentrate on his general behavior before attempting to deal with any specific difficulty. If you will take the time and effort to get him better behaved in general, then the mealtime, bedtime, or toileting problem will be much, much easier to deal with.

17

Bedtime Problems

Practically every parent has had problems getting a child to go to bed. Perhaps this problem is so common because infants usually have two naps in addition to nighttime sleeping. That means that there are three opportunities a day to have problems. It also means that there are three opportunities each day to teach your child how you want him to go to bed so you *won't* have problems.

If your child is going to bed at approximately the same time each night, give or take fifteen to twenty minutes, and she is only fussing or carrying on for five, maybe ten minutes, then you're not likely to improve much on that. If, however, your child is conning you into getting drinks, going to the bathroom, and stalling bedtime for forty-five minutes or more, you can greatly simplify your life by following the suggestions in this chapter.

The guidelines that follow will help you avoid hassling with your child at bedtime. For most parents, the only time they have alone together is the time between when the children are down for the night and when the parents go to sleep. Don't let the little ones ruin this time for you.

Prevention

Virtually all infants and young children must *learn* how to go to sleep alone. This usually requires that they learn to use objects or things in their environments as *transition objects,* which help them make the transition from being awake to being asleep. Typical transition objects are the baby's hand (sucking on the thumb, fingers, or side of the hand), a blanket (holding it up against the side of the face or sucking on the edge of it), or some stuffed toy. With any one of these transition objects, the child learns to relax with the object and fall asleep.

If the transition involves a parent, however, as in feeding to sleep, rocking to sleep, or lying down with the child until he falls asleep, the adult's presence becomes essential for sleep to occur. If the child should have any difficulty falling asleep at bedtime or in the middle of the night, then the adult must be there to get things moving along.

The easiest way to prevent bedtime problems at about three months of age is to begin placing your baby in bed awake but drowsy, providing him with several potential transition objects and allowing him (that is, leaving him alone) to learn to fall asleep by himself. If your child hasn't learned to go asleep alone, then you will need to begin this teaching. The older the child, though, the more difficult this is to do.

If you have taught your child that bed is where you go to sleep, then on those occasions when she's really fussy at bedtime, you'll have a clear reason to suspect that something may be wrong. If you fail to establish a regular routine, however, it will be difficult to tell the difference between fussing and not feeling well. Excessive crying is unnecessary, and can be eliminated. It wears on parents' nerves, which in turn tends to make them less effective parents.

Early Detection

How does a parent decide when they have or are starting to have a bedtime problem with a child? The best clues lie in the answers to a few basic questions: How smoothly does bedtime go? Is bedtime determined by the parent? Is bedtime consistent from day to day?

It's just human nature to want to avoid unpleasant situations. If every time you tell your children to get ready for bed they immediately start stalling or whining, you'll begin to try to avoid this situation. A common solution is to let the children stay up until *they* are ready to go to bed. If this is already happening in your home, then you have bedtime problems. In this instance, two of the clues are present: you're allowing the children to determine bedtime and bedtime doesn't really go smoothly.

It's easy for parents to deny that they have bedtime problems with their children, at least until things get completely out of hand. Just remember that the longer you let problems go uncorrected, the longer they take to remedy. It may be quite difficult for you to admit that very young children present bedtime problems. Sometimes par-

ents may try almost any excuse rather than admit that they simply can't get their children to bed at a reasonable time. This reluctance to recognize the problem is ridiculous. When you've never been a parent before and you haven't had two minutes of training in child-rearing procedures, how can you possibly *never* make a mistake? The greatest mistake is denying that you have a problem. Admit that you are having minor problems, and do something about them. This will prevent major problems later.

Perhaps, though, you don't mind that your child acts up a fair amount at bedtime. It's your family and your decision about what is and isn't a problem. If you are not concerned about your child's bedtime behavior, you may want to skip the suggested remedy and go on to the next chapter.

Suggested Remedy

A critical component to getting a child to fall asleep alone lies in his self-quieting skills—the ability to calm himself down when he is upset. Fortunately, self-quieting skills can be taught during the day. The best and most readily available time when self-quieting skills are necessary occurs during a time-out. Before you even begin to deal with a bedtime problem, be absolutely certain that your child is going to time-out frequently during the day and quieting himself easily. These self-quieting skills used during time-out will be very useful at sleep times.

The second major consideration in bedtime problems is fatigue. Most children do not get much hard, vigorous exercise during the day—hence, when put to bed they aren't tired enough to go to sleep. The two best exercises for children are walking and swimming. Both can and should be done with a parent and both really tire a child out.

A third important point is that children with bedtime problems should be put to bed at night and awakened in the morning at the same time, seven days a week. This will help to get them on a schedule and will usually improve their sleeping, eating, and toileting.

Begin with the day training and stay at it at least one week before you begin to work on the bedtime problem. The first night after your week of day training, start by doing whatever you usually do prior to bedtime—a bath, a bedtime story, a glass of milk and a cookie, it really doesn't matter. Change one thing, though: about thirty minutes before the bedtime you've decided upon, discourage roughhousing and running around the house. This allows your child time to slow down before going to bed.

When bedtime comes, place the child in bed, tuck him in, give him a kiss or whatever you usually do, say goodnight, tell him you'll see him in the morning, walk out of the room (I also prefer closing the door, but that's optional), and *do not* go back into the room before the next morning for anything short of a catastrophe. The first night you can expect anywhere from fifteen minutes to several hours of crying, yelling, and screaming. However, the better you do your day preparation, the easier the night training will be for both you and your child.

A slightly different problem, the child who goes to bed without incident but who wakes up in the middle of the night and cannot get back to sleep alone, is also handled by the day training described above. If you've done the day training for at least one week and your child has shown improvement during the day, then the middle-of-the-night training shouldn't take more than a couple of days to manage. The remedy for middle-of-the-night awakenings, after you've done the day training, is to ignore the child's crying, pleading, moaning, etc., and allow him to learn how to go back to sleep alone.

For a child who gets up from bed and takes off through the house, the only remedy is to pick him up and carry him back to bed without saying a single word, each and every time he gets up. (Even the child who holds our record of getting up seventy-two times prior to our intervention only got up ten times that first night.) If the problem persists, you may have to add one spank on the bottom. The child should be carried facing away from you, without a single word uttered, and gently placed back into bed. This time there's no kiss, no tucking in, and no saying goodnight. Just place the child in bed and leave the room. Within a week you should have resolved the bedtime problem and should not need to spank the child at bedtime again.

A variation on this is the child who gets up in the middle of the night, tiptoes ever so gently into his parents' room, and then joins them for the rest of the night. (Some people believe this has something to do with the need for security.) If this happens with your child, it's usually because two things are working against you: you are a sound sleeper and your child is a good creeper. Both can be handled with an ingenious little device available at most hardware or dime stores—a cowbell.

Tie the cowbell above the child's door or your door so that when the child opens the door to sneak into your room, the bell will swing down and make enough racket to awaken you. Catch the child, give him *one* spank on the bottom, and carry him back to bed, facing away from you, without saying a single word. (It does not seem plausible that nighttime roaming is caused by a security hangup when a bell hanging above the door can eliminate the problem in less than a week.) The use of a cowbell also works for children who get up at night for other reasons, such as to go to the kitchen for a midnight snack.

Sometimes children who have never been difficult at bedtime will develop a bedtime problem when recovering from an illness or hospitalization. Some will get over the problem on their own within a week after the illness subsides. However, if the problem persists more than a week, you have a bedtime problem and you may as well treat it while it's still minor. If, while you are going through the recommended procedures for eliminating bedtime problems, your child develops an illness, discontinue the procedure until the illness passes.

Once a child is self-quieting easily and frequently, is getting lots of exercise, and is on a routine schedule, bedtime problems will almost resolve themselves. The written handouts on bedtime problems at the back of this book summarize the steps to go through to remedy bedtime problems. However, with bedtime problems, as with other common behavior problems, it's assumed when remedies are discussed that you will also follow the other guidelines offered in this book. Remember, at least half of eliminating any problem behavior is catching your child being good when he is good, which usually covers a major portion of the waking day. If you aren't working on following the other guidelines, then these bedtime remedies may very well be a waste of your time.

When to Seek Professional Help

The parents of the two children who hold our clinic records for getting out of bed (seventy-two times) and crying in the middle of the night (eight hours) both required help in eliminating their respective problems. These record-holders are two examples of bedtime problems that are best handled with professional consultation. Any time a child is getting up more than twenty to thirty times or crying for more than one-and-a-half hours, the parents need help. In our outpatient clinic, this usually means two clinic appointments and a number of evening phone calls. The clinic appointments are to make certain there aren't more serious problems, and the phone calls are to help parents stick to the treatment procedures.

If your child usually goes to sleep anywhere but in bed, then you have a problem. It is not reasonable to expect a parent to hold and cuddle a child to sleep (unless the child is ill). This is too much to ask of the parent and has no practical benefit for the child. Letting a child nurse to sleep, on either breast or bottle, is equally unnecessary. In each case I've seen, the parents were just reluctant to admit they had a bedtime problem. If a child is going to bed with a bottle, unless your family doctor specifically recommends otherwise, the bottle should contain only water. Going to sleep with a bottle of milk stuck in the mouth can have a disastrous effect on a baby's teeth.

If you seek professional help and the professional wants to see either you or your child repeatedly, for a long time—try the procedures described here for a month first. If they work, you've saved yourself what could be quite a sum of money; if they don't work, you've lost only a month's time.

18

Toilet Training

Toilet training has become a parent-child battleground. There are many other skills that parents teach their children, but either friends, neighbors, and relatives don't pay any attention to whether the child has acquired those skills or the child's parents can easily make up excuses. Not so with toilet training. Many otherwise reasonable people will put pressure on parents to get their child toilet trained. At social functions, I marvel at the "records" I hear from parents. If one parent says her daughter was trained at eighteen months, someone else in the group will say that her son was potty trained at fifteen months, and on and on until some parent says that her child was potty trained at eight months. Nonsense. How can you be potty trained before you can walk to the toilet?

Some parents give children "bombardier training." After a meal, usually breakfast, the parent takes the eight-month-old into the bathroom, takes off her diaper and holds her over the toilet. When the child has a bowel movement it makes a direct hit in the toilet, and the parent has now set a record for the age at which the child was trained as a bombardier. Of course, if the parent ever forgets to hold the child over the toilet, then there'll be a bowel movement in the diaper, but that's beside the point. Or is it? What's so important about getting an eight-month-old to have bowel movements in the toilet? I have never seen or heard of an eight-month-old going to the toilet completely unassisted, and that is what toilet training is all about.

A variation on this theme is what you can call "grunt training." For this, teach your children to grunt and pull on your leg when they have to use the bathroom. Hurry them into the bathroom, take off their pants, set them on the toilet or potty chair, and they go in the toilet. Toilet trained? No! The parent is, but the child is not. With both bombardier training and grunt training, the parents, not the child, are being trained. Why not just wait until the child is ready?

107

Another technique involves setting the child on the toilet or potty chair until he or she has a bowel movement. Have you ever tried to produce a bowel movement when you didn't have to? Then why ask your child to? Giving cookies really won't help either— unless you give them enough to cause a bowel movement, which is an awful lot of cookies. There are other minor variations on this theme, too, including reading books and singing songs while the child sits on the potty chair.

If you have to go through all or some of these things to get a child toilet trained, you're starting too soon—the child's not old enough to be potty trained. Almost without exception, when we see a child of three or four years in the clinic (I've actually seen them up to fifteen and sixteen) for problems with wetting or soiling their pants during the day, it's because the parents started too early and used techniques that no one would use to teach anyone anything (except perhaps toilet training).

Thus we come to the question of how do you know when your child is "ready" to be toilet trained? This leads us to preventing problems in toilet training.

Prevention

As already indicated, toilet training that's delayed until after the child is ready will prevent many problems and much frustration. A child is *not* ready to be toilet trained just because your friends or relatives begin to ask you when you're going to toilet train him. When pressed, you need to say, firmly but nicely, "When he's ready," and drop it.

There's an excellent book that describes how to tell when a child is ready to be toilet trained. It's called *Toilet Training in Less Than a Day,* by Nathan Azrin and Richard Foxx (published by Simon & Schuster, 1974). They describe what they call their "readiness criteria," and I know of no better ones. Their criteria concern these four points:

1. Does the child have the manual dexterity to raise and lower his pants? If he doesn't, it is too soon to completely toilet train him. (This automatically eliminates some of the toilet training techniques described above.) When children are first toilet trained, there is only a short lag between the time they feel the urge to urinate or defecate and when they can't wait any longer. That is why your child should be able

to *quickly* lower his or her pants before you begin your training.

2. Does the child urinate only a couple of times a day, completely emptying his bladder, or does he still urinate a little bit many times a day? It is much easier to train a child who usually urinates four times a day than one who urinates seven or ten times because he has matured physically and has a larger capacity bladder.

3. Does he have sufficient vocabulary to understand the words connected with toilet training? This includes words like *wet, dry, pants,* and *potty.* If your child doesn't know what you're talking about, how can you toilet train him?

4. Does the child understand and follow simple commands like "Come here, please" and "Sit down"? This criterion is probably the most important of the four. Many parents think their child is good at following instructions, but they never ask her to follow any. Some parents do practically everything for a child and yet report that they aren't having any problems with the child following instructions. The question here is "Does he follow reasonable instructions *when* he's asked to?" If your child is having problems with temper tantrums whenever you direct him to do something, the chances of being able to toilet train him are very slim.

The rule of thumb I give is to wait three months after your child can successfully meet each of Azrin and Foxx's four "readiness criteria," which provides a safety margin in case you have overestimated your child's abilities. This also means that most parents won't be starting to toilet train their child until he or she is between twenty-four and thirty months. Remember that no problems are created by waiting two years to toilet train a child. In fact, if you wait long enough, they may toilet train themselves and save you all the trouble.

Early Preparations

You might as well begin early letting the little one come into the bathroom when you have to urinate (he'll probably come in anyway). Tell him that "Mommy's going pee pee in the potty" or that "Daddy is urinating in the toilet." You may choose other words, but in time your child will come to associate the words you use in your family with the various aspects of toileting behavior.

By paying close attention to the readiness criteria, you can begin teaching your child some of the skills necessary for toilet training before you actually begin to train him. For example, you can begin by teaching your son how to raise and lower his pants when you are dressing and undressing him. At first, you can pull his pants down with little or no help from him. Gradually do less and less of the pulling, letting him do more and more. This takes several weeks to accomplish. Place your hands on top of his hands and put both his hands and your hands on the top band of his pants. After you have helped him in this fashion, you will begin to feel him helping with the pulling. If you teach your child to place one hand in front and one hand in the back, it is much easier for him to get his pants up. If you haven't noticed already, small children have very prominent bottoms; therefore, if they try to lift their pants by gripping the sides, the back of their pants always gets stuck. Haven't you seen countless little people coming out of the bathroom holding their pants up with both hands, with the waistband caught right below their bottoms?

Problems in toilet training sometimes arise because a child won't follow simple instructions. Before you start the actual toilet training, you should be working on getting your child to follow instructions. The reason most parents avoid this is because if they tell their child to do something and he won't do it, they are faced with clear evidence that he won't mind them. So, instead of teaching him to mind, they just stop asking him to do things. Parents sometimes report that their child is good at following instructions, yet when I ask them to get their child to do something they say, "Oh, he doesn't like to do that." Getting a child to do only what he wants to do doesn't require skill or training. It's getting them to do something they don't want to do that tells the tale. If you attempt to toilet train a child who will not follow simple verbal instructions, you stand a very good chance of meeting with complete failure or with toilet training lasting for six or eight months.

Once you are certain your child meets the four readiness criteria discussed above and you have taught your child how to perform some of the skills involved, the way you go about the actual training makes little difference. If you want to put the potty chair in the bathroom for a week or two before you attempt training, as Dr. Spock recommends, fine. That can't hurt anything and it might help your child accept the potty chair. You must decide whether you want to use a commercially available potty chair or the toilet fixture in the bathroom.

If you decide to use the bathroom toilet, get a step or a stool the child can use both to get up onto the seat and as a place to put his feet when using the toilet. A potty chair that sits on the floor is more stable and allows the child good footing when trying to have a bowel movement. (If you want really appreciate what a small child goes through, next time you are in a restroom equipped for handicapped persons, one with a much wider door and a toilet that is raised up to make transfer from a wheelchair easier, try to have a bowel movement on that toilet. As soon as you sit on the toilet, you feel your legs dangle at the side. When you can't place your feet on the floor, you'll better understand the suggestion for using a potty chair.)

Children should not be forced to use a potty chair before they are ready. Parents too often place a child on a potty chair and say they must sit there until they have a bowel movement. That is ridiculous. Adults are not expected to have bowel movements on com-

mand. If your child gives some sign that he needs to use the bath-room (this can be anything from grimacing, to squatting down, to pulling at his pants), a sign that in the past has been followed by urinating or defecating in his diaper, then you can suggest that he sit on the potty chair. If you place importance on correct toileting (while ignoring accidents as much as possible), you'll find that both you and your child are easier to get along with.

Instead of forcing your child to sit on the potty chair for long periods of time, have him sit on the potty chair many times in one day for short periods. Even though it can be done, few parents have completely toilet trained their child in half a day, so you probably shouldn't count on it. Spend the first weekend using intensive train-ing procedures, but a weekend may not be long enough. Some par-ents have spent over a year toilet training their child, so don't get your hopes up that you're going to be able to toilet train your child in less than a day. Plan on several weeks of practice with your child and up to six months of teaching before he is completely accident free.

You may want to spend five minutes with your child after each correct bowel movement in the toilet, doing (within reason) some-thing with the child that the child chooses to do. That helps the child learn that doing something his *parent* wants leads to doing something *he* wants. Don't, however, resort to punishment if you find that a month or two after toilet training your child starts having accidents again. (Remember—punishment does not teach what you want the child to learn.) Instead, spend a little extra time with your child teaching her the way you want things done, and when she does it correctly, spend time with her letting her know you appreciate it.

When to Seek Professional Help

It's common for children in the three- to five- or six-year-old range to occasionally have urinary accidents when they're outside playing or intently involved in something. This really isn't a prob-lem unless it's happening once every two weeks or more.

If you have a child who is frequently constipated, you should contact your doctor. Home remedies for constipation, such as sup-positories, enemas, or laxatives, should not normally be given to children without a doctor's advice. If you cannot relieve constipation with fairly simple dietary changes, you need your doctor's reassur-ance that your child is physically all right and her suggestions on

how to prevent future constipation. Some children alternate constipation with soiling. They'll go two, three, or four days without a
bowel movement, soil, then go several days more. If your child fits
this pattern, take her to your doctor.

Diarrhea, if it persists for more than two days or occurs often,
means you should see your physician. Home remedies sometimes
make the diarrhea worse—even though you might think that whatever you're giving for it is producing an improvement. Diarrhea in a
child less than one year of age should be reported to your doctor
without delay. This can be serious—don't put it off.

If your child is still having bowel movements in his pants at the
age of four years, see your physician. Soiling can frequently be rem-
edied easily, so don't delay treatment. As mentioned previously, I
have seen children in the clinic who were still soiling at fifteen and
sixteen years of age; this is far too long to wait. If you go to one
doctor for the soiling and the treatment fails to help within one
month, you'd better see another doctor.

19

Eating Problems

Eating problems usually come to the attention of the pediatrician or the family physician only after the parents find that their child's behavior in restaurants is totally unacceptable or when they become concerned about their child's physical growth. However, almost every parent experiences occasional difficulties that may not be serious but are still aggravating.

Some children develop serious aversions to certain food. Meats frequently fall into this category. If your child gags and occasionally vomits when you try to introduce any particular food, you need to check with your doctor. Children who consistently vomit at mealtime need professional help. Also, if you're not getting behavior as dramatic as vomiting but still find yourself limited to a very small number of foods that your child will eat, you are having significant mealtime problems.

Some children insist upon having the same foods over and over again (examples that come to mind were two children who insisted on having applesauce and mashed potatoes at each meal). Parents who experience this problem, not over just a week or two but over two to three months, should get professional help.

Mealtime problems, even serious ones, are relatively easy to treat. If your doctor tells you that "your child will outgrow it," you'd better schedule an appointment with another pediatrician for a second opinion. The cost of an office call is a small price to pay for the peace of mind that comes with a second opinion.

The age at which a child begins solid foods, eats with her fingers, or learns to use a spoon is less important than having her enjoy mealtime and eat a variety of foods. Later on, making meals a time for family social interaction is very important. Pleasant mealtime conversation should involve all members of a family. This does more to make mealtimes into family times than does anything else.

Prevention

There's no way to completely avoid eating problems, but there are a number of things you can do to reduce the chances of having them. You may find, as you introduce new foods to your child, that he will act as though he doesn't like them. This is because they taste different from what he is used to; it's no big deal. A very young child, when you just begin to spoon-feed him, has a beautiful way of telling you that he doesn't like something. When you put a foreign-tasting food in his mouth, he opens his mouth, sticks out his tongue, closes his lips around his tongue, then retracts his tongue, leaving the foreign-tasting material to dribble down his front. He may also make grimaces that lead you to believe you really put something foul-tasting in his mouth.

The best way to handle this situation is to feed the child several spoonsful of a food that he is used to, then try a small spoonful of the new food again, fully expecting him to spit it out. Do this throughout the meal, alternating several spoonsful of familiar foods with the unfamiliar one. After several tries he'll accept the new food as if he'd been eating it all along. Whatever you do, don't try to physically force your child to eat something he doesn't want. Just take it slow and be patient.

Also, when feeding your child, make sure you are talking to him and smiling at him every time he swallows a bit of food. This allows him to slowly get used to new-tasting foods while he learns that eating is a fun time when Dad and Mom do a lot of talking and smiling.

Early Preparations

When eating problems are developing, your child will gradually reduce the variety of foods he'll accept or make a big fuss when you try to feed him something he has refused before. If you find yourself feeding a very small number of foods, chances are you're seeing early signs of eating problems.

Food allergies have received much attention over the last few years. For a time, nearly every child who came into our clinic with any kind of behavior problem was thought to be allergic to something, if not everything. Granted, some children do have food allergies. But it's cheaper to spend some time and effort trying to deal with the situation as if it were an eating problem before you start the allergy test series. I don't know of many allergic reactions that involve crying and screaming at the *sight* of a particular food.

Your family doctor is your best choice if you are convinced or just concerned that your child is allergic to certain foods. Your doctor will probably suggest that you eliminate suspected foods for a week or two and then put them back in your child's diet. If the allergic reaction (rash or hives, swelling, itching) returns after eating the suspected foods, then the allergy tests are probably in order.

Suggested Remedy

First, be certain your child isn't gaining attention from you by being a problem eater. If you're coaxing and trying to con her into eating certain foods while she fusses and pushes them away, you'll probably never win. One clever thing that you can try, both to get your child to eat the new food and to rule out any chance that she has an allergy to it, is to mix a small amount of the new food with a large amount of a favorite food until you can't see it any more. Be sure to use a small enough quantity of the new food that even *you* can't taste it when you know it's there. Gradually increase the amount of the new food until you have fifty-fifty mix. If this still does not produce an adverse reaction, you can rest assured that your child is not allergic to the new food and you can increase the mix more quickly until you're feeding the new food full strength.

When some parents complain of a child's poor eating habits, the problem is that the child is filling up on junk foods between meals. These snacks and sweets are expensive, usually not very nutritious, and dramatically affect a child's appetite. If this is your child's problem, the solution is to never buy these foods. If you can't live without junk foods yourself, then you're half the problem.

If you are having problems with your child at mealtime or if he simply does not seem to be able to gain weight, there are some changes you can make that really can't hurt your child and may be a big help:

1. Make sure that you offer three or four discrete meals at about the same time every day. The more worried you are about the problem, the more rigidly you should keep the feeding schedule you set.

2. Get your child vigorous exercise every day. This might consist of long walks or playing hard with Mom or Dad. However, as noted in a previous chapter, playing within the house usually is not enough exercise to really count.

3. Do not offer your child food or liquids between regularly scheduled meals. How can he possibly build up an appetite if you do? Many well-intentioned parents will make juices and other snacks available between meals in an attempt to get extra calories into their children. This is almost always counterproductive. If you want to improve a child's appetite, then you need to ensure extended periods of time without any food or liquids.

4. Keep your child's sleep schedule about the same every day, with no more than thirty minutes' variation in awake and asleep times. There's nothing like a good schedule to help to improve appetite.

Slow Eating

Some parents tell me that their child just pokes at his food and seems to take forever to get a meal down. Home visits in these situations inevitably show two things:

1. The child is allowed to eat junk between meals, sometimes right before a meal; and

2. The parents give the child a great deal of attention in trying to get him to eat his food in a reasonable time.

The best recourse in this situation is the small timer you use when you put your child in the chair for time-out. Set the timer so you know that he could eat the food in the time allotted (twenty-five minutes for lunch, for example). Tell him that if he is not finished with his lunch when the bell rings, you will remove his lunch and he won't get anything to eat until the next meal. Stick to what you tell him. Do *not* talk to him, smile at him, or pay any attention to him except when he is actually eating. Then you can frequently, briefly, catch him being good and offer him love pats. You will find (if you make sure he doesn't sneak into your junk food supply when you're not watching) that in a few days your child is much better at eating in the time allotted. Gradually reduce the allotted time until he has the same amount of time as others in the family.

When to Seek Professional Help

If your child is not gaining weight properly, you should contact your doctor. Children's food intake frequently drops off dramatically at about one year of age. But even with this, their appetite continues and their weight gain, although reduced, should be constant.

20

Dressing Problems

At approximately one year of age children begin trying to help dress themselves. By the time they can completely dress themselves, they may be four to five years old. What this means is that you have a good, three-year job ahead of you, so you best not let dressing problems get the upper hand. During this time you'll go through phases where your child insists on dressing without help and gets angry during the process. You'll find shirts and pants put on backwards; a crying child with one arm through a sleeve or his head barely jammed through the opening; and occasionally, to add a little excitement to your life, you'll find him running around stark naked, laughing and obviously enjoying life. These are all very normal behaviors, so don't get uptight about them—not when you still have several years of learning and teaching ahead of you.

Prevention

The chapter "Let Them Help You" discussed encouraging your child to help in getting herself dressed. You can pull pants most of the way up and let your child finish the job. Or, you can pull a shirt most of the way over her head and let her pull it the rest of the way. The point is that you want getting dressed to be a pleasant time for your child. Talk to her while you're dressing her—not just about getting dressed, but about whatever comes into your mind. This is a good time to get some extra hugs, too. Hugs, by the way, have a way of decreasing as children get older. Parents usually miss them. So get all the hugs you can while your child still gives them freely.

When your child shows an interest in dressing, try to assist by seeing that shirts, socks, and pants are large enough to be pulled on easily. This also means that they can be pulled off easily, but that's going to happen anyway, so try to accept it. As your child attempts dressing, don't be stingy with your love pats and encouragement.

118

Keep giving feedback on what a nice job he's doing or how quickly he got started. Getting dressed by yourself when you're small can be a frustrating experience, so parents should provide plenty of encouragement.

Early Detection

Some frustration and some tears are to be expected, but out-and-out temper tantrums are too much. Watch, also, for stubborn refusal to wear new clothes or certain jackets, shirts, or pants. It's all right for children to have some preferences among their clothing, but don't let your little one make the selection process a power struggle.

If you find that at the age of four you're still providing a lot of help with shirts, dresses, or pants, you have a dressing problem and dressing problems are typically *not* outgrown—they just get worse. Shoes are a different story, though. Children usually learn everything about dressing before they learn how to tie shoes, so don't push it. You may want to just purchase a pair of cowboy boots. They're easy to slip on and off, which is particularly nice when your little one comes in with muddy feet—no muddy shoestrings. Shoes with velcro fasteners also present a convenient alternative. Your child can learn to tie his shoes later.

Another sign of possible trouble is stalling. Stalling is a favorite tactic of children who have a relatively short time to get ready in the morning. If you come in to see how your son is doing and he's sitting on his bed in his pajamas, this makes you angry, and you frequently have to really rush to keep from being late to work or to get him to school.

Suggested Remedies

The easiest way to work on stalling is to pick times when it doesn't matter to you how long your child stalls. For example, instead of working on getting dressed in the morning, when you know you're going to end up late for work or school, start out working on getting ready for bed. Ask your child to get his pj's on at seven o'clock if you want him in bed by eight. If he doesn't begin immediately, send him to time-out. That way, he can go to time-out fifteen times in the hour before bedtime, or he can get his pj's on and have an enjoyable hour to spend with you. If he isn't ready for bed at the end of the hour, carry him in to bed, take off his shoes, and put him to bed in his clothes. Once you get your child ready for bed in a timely fashion, dressing at other times should be much easier.

Many parents will find that they really run into trouble when they are trying to meet a tight time schedule with their children. Dressing certainly has the potential to create one of these troubled situations. For almost all time-limited problems, such as trying to get children off to preschool or school on time, there are several things that you can try out:

1. Practice compliance (getting your child to do what he's told shortly after he's told to do it) during times when it is not important that the task be done quickly, as described above in the suggestions for dealing with stalling.

2. The instant that your child decides to start getting ready for bed, provide him with a lot of good love pats (time-in). Try to have a snack or a favorite story ready for him the minute he's ready for bed.

3. Look for other times during the week when you can work on general compliance. For example, on Saturday you might ask your daughter to get her coat on so you can go to the store. If she doesn't get moving, put her in time-out where she cannot see her favorite television show. Repeat this request until she complies. You, in turn, probably have a hundred things that you can do while she's in time-out.

4. In situations where you simply do not have the luxury of time, such as in the morning, always have a contingency plan. For example, with regard to getting dressed in time to go to preschool, insist that your child get dressed *first,* then eat, and then watch television. Any refusal to get dressed or to eat should result in an immediate time-out. Compliance should be followed immediately with love pats.

When children have to get off to preschool or to a day-care center, you might wait to serve breakfast until they are dressed. You can start this when they're two-and-a-half, so they're used to it by the time they're old enough to go to school. Talk to the preschool or day-care teacher ahead of time so the teacher knows what you're up to. Then tell your child very matter-of-factly that if he isn't dressed in time for breakfast, you'll dress him and take him to school without breakfast. This usually requires only a few days, which isn't nearly long enough for malnutrition to set in, but it is long enough for your child to figure out that you aren't kidding.

Some teachers, for reasons I don't understand, refuse to cooperate with this procedure and insist on feeding your poor "starving" child a snack as soon as he gets to school. Small children soon figure out who these pushovers are and then work them for sympathy. Such teachers are often the same ones who suggest something ridiculous like "You need to have a talk with your son"; they should read the chapter on lectures.

Dressing problems are compounded by letting children get dressed while they watch television. Why not switch it around? Don't allow them to watch television until after they're dressed, have their rooms picked up, and their beds made. This may take some effort on your part for a week or two (maybe more), but it's well worth it in the long run.

If you need to use the discipline chair for behavior problems during dressing, don't be reluctant. The sooner you enforce the rules, the sooner the problems will be under control. If your child acts up while dressing and has to sit in the chair a couple of times, this will only delay what he likes to do, which should motivate him to get dressed.

When to Seek Professional Help

Unfortunately, most professionals don't have much experience dealing with dressing problems. If your child is having serious tantrums, or he has reached age four and is still unable to dress himself, you probably need to go to a medical center teaching hospital for an evaluation. If the behavior problems during dressing are serious, then chances are your child is experiencing some other serious behavior problems as well. You need someone who can help you with all of them.

21

Bedwetting

Pediatricians as well as lay people are finally admitting that some normal children who are five, six, or even seven years old still wet their beds. Often, one or both parents have a history of bedwetting until reaching a similar age. For unknown reasons, more boys than girls tend to be bedwetters.

Most parents worry about bedwetting before it is actually a clinical problem. I don't consider bedwetting a problem until it begins to interfere with the child's social life. If your son is afraid to go on a camping trip or stay at a friends's house or with relatives, then he's old enough for you to do something about the bedwetting. This doesn't usually occur until the child is eight to ten years old. Many parents worry about bedwetting when their children are four or five years of age, which is too early. Don't concern yourself with bedwetting until your child is at least six or seven.

Prevention

Although I don't know any way to prevent bedwetting, there are some things that parents *should not do* if they have a bedwetter. First, don't make a fuss every morning you find a wet bed. Bedwetters are very sound sleepers and don't discover for themselves that they've wet the bed until the next morning. Games like refusing liquids to the child after dinner, waking him up when you go to bed (so he can go to the bathroom), or setting an alarm clock for the middle of the night only make your child more sensitive about bedwetting.

When I say that I don't consider bedwetting a problem, I mean you shouldn't do *anything* about it until six or seven years of age. If you have a child nine, ten, or twelve years old who wets the bed and it doesn't bother you—fine. If you can ignore the bedwetting, I doubt seriously that it will harm your child. On the other hand, there are some home remedies for bedwetting that can cause bitter feelings between parents and child. Don't let yourself get caught in the trap of ridiculing your child or, worse yet, spanking him or taking away privileges for wetting the bed. To do so will only make you hate each other. I don't know of any case where such tactics have stopped the bedwetting.

One thing for certain is that children do not wet the bed because they are insecure—insecurity doesn't often go along with sleeping like a rock. Insecure persons usually keep waking up to make sure everything is still all right. All the bedwetters I've worked with have been very sound sleepers. There's one thing to keep in ming, though: if you make a big enough fuss over the bedwetting, over a long enough period of time, *you* can make your child insecure. But then it's not the bedwetting that's the problem, it's you.

Suggested Remedies

In addition to a complete physical examination by your family doctor, you should know if your child has problems with daytime urinary incontinence (trickles or wets his pants during the day) and whether he has trouble with bowel functioning. If either of these conditions is present, you need to mention them to your family doctor when you take your child in for the examination.

There are two or three treatment procedures that have reportedly helped stop bedwetting. Unfortunately, I know of no studies that have compared these treatment procedures, and only one of them can be used by parents without professional help. My preferred treatment, if you can stand it, is to wait until your child stops wetting the bed on his own. However, commercially available bedwetting alarms sometimes work (both Montgomery Ward and Sears have offered these through their catalogs). Research indicates that the alarms work with about 80 percent of the children they're used with, but the relapse rate is high, almost 50 percent. This means that even if the alarm works, you have an even chance that your child will start wetting the bed again, at which time you must start using the bedwetting alarm again. Also, don't look for immediate results. The alarms can take several months to work, and by then many parents have already lost patience.

The other methods referred to cannot be implemented without professional guidance. Some children stop wetting the bed after their diet is changed to eliminate foods to which they are allergic, but this requires the help of a pediatric allergist and won't necessarily be successful. Other doctors have reported success with hypnosis. This is certainly not something that should be tried without a good physical examination first, and then hypnosis should be done only by a qualified hypnotist.

In a 1974 article in *Behaviour Research and Therapy,* Azrin, Sneed, and Foxx discuss procedures for curing bedwetting that have worked with most of the children with whom we have tried them. However, these procedures are complicated. Ask your doctor for the name of a good clinician who knows how to use Azrin's procedures. As a point of information, I know of no published scientific study (notice I didn't say testimonial) that has ever shown that psychotherapy of any kind stops bedwetting. If you want your child to get some psychotherapy, fine, but don't expect it to stop his bedwetting.

One final note of encouragement is in order. A number of researchers are working on this problem now. More and more procedures are being reported every year. Although right now this only serves to further confuse the issue, I think that a relatively inexpensive, practical, and effective procedure for treating bedwetting will soon be available through family doctors. If you are going to try any expensive procedures, be certain that the person you are working with is licensed to practice in your state. Check with your child's pediatrician or your family doctor. If you're still in doubt, check with a teaching hospital or major medical center's department of pediatrics before you agree to any treatment procedure involving a lot of money.

22

Thumbsucking

Thumbsucking is another of those common behaviors often said to indicate an insecure child. Whoever started those rumors about insecure children must have been selling a program for working with insecure children. I have seen many children who suck their thumbs—some of them were insecure and some weren't. Insecurity doesn't account for the behavior. Thumbsucking *is* one of those behaviors, however, that friends and relatives are first to notice.

I recommend that parents put off doing anything about this until their dentist indicates that thumbsucking is going to have a bad effect on the child's teeth. The child usually outgrows the thumbsucking before his teeth are in any danger. If you haven't taken your child to a dentist by the time he's three years old, he probably has a worse problem than thumbsucking—cavities.

Suggested Remedy

If the dentist indicates that it's time to stop the thumbsucking, it is important to remember that you are working on a *habit.* Your child is not intentionally sucking his thumb. He has become used to the habit and usually doesn't realize he is doing it. If you want to eliminate the habit, you must avoid the temptation to nag, threaten, or lecture.

When you begin the procedures to eliminate the thumbsucking, make certain that you start at a time when you have at least two days (like a weekend) when your child will be with you, not at preschool or with a baby-sitter. Make the days as pleasant as possible, except for the thumbsucking. Every time the thumbsucking occurs, paint the child's thumb or fingers with a foul-tasting commercial compound, such as "StopZit" (available from most pharmacies without a prescription), and use the time-out chair. Place the child

125

on a chair for two or three minutes (don't forget to use the portable timer), don't criticize him, and when the time is up, let him get up. It usually takes several days before the habit is broken. If you notice the habit recurring, start the procedures over again immediately.

There is a written handout at the back of this book that summarizes these procedures, which were evaluated by our office and published in *Pediatrics* (a journal for pediatricians) in 1986.

Other Considerations

23

Grandparents

Grandparents are nice, well-intentioned, sincere child spoilers. The effects of this spoiling, unless repeated at frequent intervals, will not be permanent.

The fewer problems grandparents cause, the more they should be encouraged to interact with their grandchildren. If you are forced into a showdown with your parents over your child-rearing procedures, you really have no choice but to do what you think best for your child. Your parents were allowed some mistakes with you, and you should be afforded the same privilege. If grandparents try to force you, or coerce you, into toilet training before you think your child is ready, or give you advice about too many of the day-to-day activities you engage in with your child, ask them as tactfully as you can to please leave the choices up to you.

If this doesn't work, you should take a stronger position, even at the risk of offending your parents. Chances are that whatever you do will be less offensive the sooner you do it. The worst thing you can do is to allow a disagreement to go on and on. Most grandparents, if told off nicely, will realize that you are not against them. Be careful not to alienate them if you can avoid it. Remember, your parents had to survive sixteen to eighteen years or more with you before they could enjoy grandparenthood. You will probably want to turn to them sometime for help or advice they can provide as well or better than anyone else.

Do not move into your parent's home with your child or children if you can avoid it. If you do move in, move out as soon as possible. Accept no monetary support from your parents if you can avoid that. If you have to borrow from them, borrow only what is absolutely necessary and pay it back as quickly as possible. There are few things more upsetting to parents than the fear that they raised a real loser. Even if you're a temporary loser, try not to let them know it—don't move in and don't ask them to pay your bills.

Finally, try to avoid the temptation to abuse your parents by making them baby-sit with your child(ren) every time that you want to go out. While there's nothing wrong with your parents watching your child(ren), preferably it should be when they would like to and not just for your convenience.

24

Exceptional Kids Can Learn Too!

Many children experience some physical or medical handicap during their childhood. This is no reason for you to stop teaching the things discussed earlier in this book; it's all the *more* reason for you to work harder at teaching your child. Whether a child is retarded, exceptionally bright, suffering from cardiac problems, or whatever, to the limits prescribed his physician he should be expected to do things around the house for himself. You are doing this child a favor (over the long term) if you treat him as normally as possible, regardless of what makes him exceptional.

Too many parents use a diagnostic label, such as borderline mental retardation, as an excuse for the way their child (mis)behaves. A much healthier approach is to conclude from the diagnostic label that your child requires more teaching in order to achieve the same goals. To deny your child attainable goals is a disservice to you and the child as well as to whatever potential he or she may have for leading a normal and unrestricted life.

Interestingly, many of the procedures discussed in the preceding chapters were originally used with exceptional children. Timeout, for example, was first employed with retarded children and in institutions for emotionally disturbed children. The procedures described for toilet training and bedwetting were conducted with mentally retarded children and adults before they were adapted for use with children of normal intelligence.

There are several basic features to children's learning that apply regardless of intellectual level and regardless of medical or physical handicaps:

1. Children learn optimally when they are given many opportunities for learning. For example, whether you are trying to teach

your child the alphabet or how to behave at mealtime, the more opportunities he has to practice the faster he will learn. Just as important as the number of opportunities is the time that passes between these opportunities. Any parent who has learned to water ski or roller skate knows that, as you learn *how* to do each component, you need the opportunity to *try* what you've learned as soon as possible. Although there is a temptation to say "I don't ever want you to do that again," your child will benefit most if he has an opportunity to do it again almost immediately.

2. Ideally, a child should be presented with a dramatic contrast between what happens when he does something right and when he does it wrong. If a child receives time-in for doing things correctly and time-out for incorrect behaviors, he will learn at the maximum rate possible. With complicated tasks, it's important to break the tasks into their component parts and teach the parts before you worry about the overall task. For example, when toilet training, it's easier to teach the vocabulary words and the physical skills long before you even attempt to actually "toilet train" your child.

3. For many children, it is just as important to provide time-in or praise for starting on a task as it is to do so for completing the task. Further, it is often important to provide time-in for continuing on the task as well.

4. Discipline should be immediate, unemotional, and not preceded by a succession of warnings. With very few exceptions, waiting to discipline a child only prolongs the learning.

5. Discipline is best established before you need it. We often see young children hospitalized with a serious illness or injury who were essentially undisciplined before their hospitalization and thus are unable to comply with examinations, necessary treatments, and so on. While the parents probably thought that they were doing their child a favor through lax discipline, they really can make the child's life (or in this case, hospital stay) miserable by doing so.

For example, when it comes to testing a child for academic or psychological purposes, the test is usually only as good as the child's cooperation or compliance allows. If the examiner has difficulty getting the child's cooperation, it's almost impossible to determine how much the test results were influenced by this. Conversely, a very well-behaved child who cooperates fully will obtain the best possible results on any testing that is done.

School Evaluation and Placement

Every year literally tens of thousands of children are not doing well in school for one reason or another. In 1975, the federal government passed Public Law 94-142, which guarantees every child an education, regardless of any extenuating circumstances, physical, intellectual, emotional, or behavioral. This law provides that the local school district *must,* if requested by a simple letter from the parents, conduct an appropriate evaluation of the child's abilities and provide that child with an educational environment that will maximize his learning.

If the school district cannot provide either the evaluation or the classroom placement, it must pay to have the evaluation and the education done elsewhere. Some personnel in school districts fail to inform parents of their right to a free evaluation by the school, preferring instead to suggest, imply the need for, or actually refer the parents to a private practitioner for the evaluation. The problem with a private evaluation is that the school district is not bound by its results and the parents are responsible for any cost(s) incurred. Conversely, if the school conducts the evaluation, the recommendations from the evaluation are binding upon the school and the parents incur no financial obligation.

The school also is obligated to bring together the parents and the appropriate professionals to decide upon a written list of objectives for the child's education. Further, a date not more than one year later must be set for reviewing these objectives and the child's performance, to determine both the appropriateness of the objectives as well as the child's progress towards meeting them. These objectives and the time frame constitute an Individualized Education Plan or IEP, as it's come to be known.

Thus, whether your child is retarded, is gifted, or has severe medical problems, the school district has legal obligations to him; specifically, to evaluate and then to provide an educational placement in accordance with that evaluation that will, in the opinion of the professionals involved, provide the best education possible.

25

Seeking Professional Help

If you have serious concerns, either after reading this book or independent of it, seek the services of a board certified pediatrician. You can find out from your county medical society, a local hospital, or from any good reference library who the board certified pediatricians are in your area. Although being board certified is no guarantee that your doctor can answer all your questions, it does guarantee that he or she has completed at least three years of study in pediatrics *after* receiving the M.D. degree and has passed both written and oral exams in pediatrics.

If the board certified pediatrician cannot solve your problem, he or she should recommend someone who can. Where children are concerned, it is always best to start with a certified pediatrician rather than a mental health center or a privately practicing psychiatrist, psychologist, or social worker. The pediatrician can then refer you to someone known to be good at dealing with childhood behavior problems.

When you seek professional help for your child, there are several questions you should ask. Although they may make you feel uncomfortable, you may save yourself considerable heartbreak as well as money if you ask them. What kind of training and experience does this professional have with children? College degrees (the M.D. and the Ph.D.) are no guarantee that the professional has adequate background to handle your child's problems. The fact that a professional is licensed or certified to practice in your state is good to know, but that still does not give the assurance that you need. If your pediatrician recommends a professional who is licensed to practice in your state, there is one important question left—have they seen the types of concerns that you have before? A professional who works exclusively with children is probably a better bet than one who see adults most of the time.

Find out how much each visit will cost, how many visits will probably be necessary, and over what period of time. It's common for a doctor to provide estimates of time and cost. If you are told "I don't know, these problems took years to develop and they'll probably take years to remedy," you should be suspicious. Mental health professionals used to be able to get away with that line, but fortunately parents need not settle for this anymore.

If the professional wants to "test" your child, find out why, what the tests will cost, and what they will tell you. It is not uncommon for a doctor to see you and then schedule tests that are done by a student or by an employee who holds a less advanced degree. The doctor then interprets the test. There's nothing wrong with this practice so long as you know it's going on, so don't be afraid to ask who will do the testing.

A child can sometimes be treated for less cost than he can be tested. Better find this out before you agree to the testing. Frequently, too, in the process of treating a child, the professional learns more first hand than he or she learns through testing. Don't let your guard down just because the professional says that the testing or treatment is covered by your medical insurance. So what? If the testing doesn't need to be done, or the professional isn't adequately trained to do the treatment, the fact that it is free is beside the point.

Be wary of the doctor who can treat the child's behavior problem and the parent's rocky marriage and sexual dysfunctioning with one fell swoop. It's difficult enough to treat children under ten years of age for nonorganic problems without also treating everything else that walks through the door. Doctors are sometimes pressured by the parents, who will say "You've done such a wonderful job with Jimmie, can you help us to work on some problems with our marriage?" The doctor, in most cases, should refer you to someone else.

If the doctor recommends prescription drugs to control your child's behavior, find out why, what the medicine is supposed to accomplish, what the side effects are, and how long the medicine will probably be used. If the recommendation is made by someone other than a board certified pediatrician, get a second opinion from such a pediatrician. There are some conditions, such as Attention Deficit Disorder (formerly known as hyperactivity), that respond to a combination of drugs and behavior management. There are some, such as epilepsy, that respond best to just medication. Finally, there are conditions that respond best to just behavioral management procedures (for example, oppositional behavior).

Finally, if after several weeks of treatment you don't see some change in the way your child behaves, it is possible that this doctor's treatment will never bring about observable change in your child's behavior. If your doctor says your child is changing and you just can't tell it yet, ask when he or she thinks *you'll* be able to see some improvement.

26

Concluding Remarks

Living with children is a continuous teaching and learning process for both children and parents. Almost everything a child learns during his first few years is dramatically influenced by his interaction with his parents. The important thing, and a point emphasized throughout this book, is that parents are teachers, not on selected occasions or during certain periods, but during most of the time they spend interacting with their children. The manner in which a parent handles any single interaction, whether pleasant or unpleasant, is not nearly so important as how the parent generally interacts with the child.

Child rearing gives thousands of pleasant, memorable experiences for parents, even though most adults have little formal or informal training in parenting. They just handle each day as they encounter it, hoping that somehow everything will work out all right. Most of the advice they receive is corrective. Relatives or friends often tell you what you should have done to avoid a situation that has already occurred. No matter how superb you are as a parent, you will have some disappointments that may lead you to question what you are doing. I'm advocating that you start right off working toward a pleasant, educative interaction with your child. Ignore minor setbacks. Concentrate your efforts on positive ways of building useful, pleasant behavior in your children. Treating them as adults, as little people, is the best way to do this.

Successful parenting is the most rewarding experience a person can ever expect to enjoy. The love you share with your child is a love that can't be experienced in any other way. Every day you should do everything you can to encourage, understand, nurture, and enjoy that love.

Bibliography

Azrin, N. H., and Foxx, R. M. 1974. *Toilet training in less than a day.* New York: Simon & Schuster.

Azrin, N. H., Sneed, T. J., and Foxx, R. M. 1974. Dry-bed training: Rapid elimination of childhood enuresis. *Behaviour Research and Therapy* 12:147-56.

Barnard, J. D., Christophersen, E. R., and Wolf, M. M. 1977. Teaching children appropriate shopping behavior through parent training in the supermarket setting. *Journal of Applied Behavior Analysis* 10:49-59.

Becker, W. C. 1971. *Parents are teachers: A child management program.* Champaign, IL: Research Press.

Becker, W. C., and Becker, J. W. 1974. *Successful parenthood: How to teach your child values, competence and responsibility.* Chicago: Follett.

Christophersen, E. R. 1977. Children's behavior during automobile rides: Do car seats make a difference? *Pediatrics* 60:69-74.

Christophersen, E. R. and Gyulay, J. E. 1981. Parental compliance with car seat usage: A positive approach with long-term follow-up. *Journal of Pediatric Psychology* 6(3):301-12.

Christophersen, E. R., and Rapoff, M. A. 1983. Toileting problems of children. In *Handbook of clinical child psychology,* C. E. Walker and M. C. Roberts, Eds. New York: John Wiley & Sons.

Friman, P. C., Barone, V. J., and Christophersen, E. R. 1986. Aversive taste treatment of finger and thumb sucking. *Pediatrics* 78(1):174-6.

Mathews, J. R., Friman, P. C., Barone, V. J., Ross, L. V., and Christophersen, E. R. 1987. Decreasing dangerous infant behaviors through parent instruction. *Journal of Applied Behavior Analysis* 20(2):165-9.

Quilitch, H. R., Christophersen, E. R., and Risley, T. R. 1977. Evaluation of children's play materials. *Journal of Applied Behavior Analysis* 10:501.

Rapoff, M. A., Christophersen, E. R., and Rapoff, K. E. 1982.

The management of common childhood bedtime problems by
pediatric nurse practitioners. *Journal of Pediatric Psychology*
7(2):179-96.

Spock, B. 1976. *Baby and child care.* New York: Pocket Books.

White, B. L. 1975. *The first three years of life.* Englewood Cliffs, NJ:
Prentice-Hall.

Summary Handouts

The pages that follow offer summaries of many of the procedures that were discussed in the preceding chapters as well as some that are of related interest. These step-by-step summaries are designed so that, when you decide to work on a particular problem, you'll have quick access to the guidelines elaborated on in the text. These pages are perforated so that you can easily remove them from the book for ready reference.

Coping with your child's initial resistance to any of these procedures can be trying. As parents, we instinctively feel that crying is just not good for our child and should be avoided at all costs. Not so. Sometimes the only way that we can get something done is to put up with some crying. If your daughter cries really hard for the first minute or two that she's on the time-out chair, you can rest easier if you remind yourself that she is getting a good workout for her heart and lungs.

You, in turn, need to find something to do to distract yourself so you don't lose your mind. Try reading the guidelines *aloud* to yourself while your daughter is screaming. This serves three purposes: 1) it distracts you from the crying, 2) it reminds you that you are following the procedures correctly, and 3) it helps you to ignore the crying so that the procedure will get easier and easier on both you and your child.

Other forms of distraction you might want to consider are to call your own phone number (or a time and weather number) and pretend to carry on a conversation. You can purposely wait to start the bedtime procedures until the beginning of one of your favorite TV shows. You might start the dressing procedures at a time when your son is really excited about going somewhere. And, finally, you should choose your child's favorite breakfast for the first few mornings that you go through the mealtime procedures.

Remember to pick the time carefully, for when you start a procedure, be prepared for the worst. Don't give up until you're successful and, to make both you and your child feel better and to reduce any guilt you might feel, make sure you always "catch 'em being good."

Preparing for Parenthood

1. Select the doctor you want to care for your child before your expected delivery date, and schedule at least one appointment with him or her to discuss any part of health care about which you have questions or concerns.
2. After delivery, make sure that someone teaches both mother and father the basic infant caregiving skills, such as bathing, diapering, feeding, and dressing. Both parents should have experience holding, diapering, feeding, and dressing the baby while in the hospital. If you plan to breast-feed, it's a good idea to pick a coach who has had experience with breast-feeding.
3. If you have someone (relative or friend) coming to your home to help after your delivery, ask them to help with the household tasks and let you adjust to caring for the new baby.
4. Talk to your baby while you are taking care of him. Use normal speech, not baby talk, and look at your baby's face while talking.
5. Spend time playing with and exploring your new baby. Make sure both parents get ample practice with him! Be sure to *make time* for these interactions while your baby is rested, fed, and happy.
6. Try to develop standard caregiving routines and, within reason, stick with those routines. For example, it's a good idea to use the same place and the same procedures each time you diaper or bathe your baby.
7. Work very hard to hold and play with your child when he is quiet and happy instead of waiting for him to cry. Babies learn very quickly which behaviors gain them attention.
8. You will teach your infant something each time that you interact with him, so begin very early giving attention to those things that you want your baby to do.
9. Purchase an infant car seat before your baby is discharged from the hospital and use it on every trip you make in an automobile.

From *Little People: A Commonsense Guide to Child Rearing* (3rd ed.) by Edward R. Christophersen. Published by Westport Publishers, Inc., Kansas City, MO.

Excessive Crying in Infants

Some babies seem to cry all or most of the time. Most of their parents' efforts, including cuddling them, carrying them, talking softly to them, or holding them, do not reduce the baby's crying. With these babies, attempts to let them "cry it out" don't seem to help, either. They just can't seem to be consoled. Because the procedures that we recommend usually will produce a decrease in crying within three days, there is little risk to the parent who wants to try them.

There are two sharply contrasting activities that parents can do in an effort to reduce the amount of infant crying. These procedures are best begun shortly after your baby has awakened and has been fed, burped, diapered, and generally attended to for a little while.

1. Place your baby on a blanket on the floor, near enough to you so that you can engage in an everyday activity that takes a while for you to complete. This activity could be, for example, paying the bills, reading, or doing paperwork. Stay very near your baby but *do not interact with him in any way as long as he is crying.* Just maintain your activity and wait for the second that there is a break in his crying.
2. The instant that the crying lets up, briefly rub your baby's head or back with your hand without saying a word. The second that he starts crying again, immediately go back to your activity.
3. Keep up these two contrasting actions for at least thirty minutes at a time, performing the exercise at least three times a day. If you can rub the baby's head or back for longer than one or two seconds without him crying, do so. But remember, the instant he starts crying, stop your touching.
4. When you first begin these procedures, pick your baby up at the end of a session immediately following a quiet spell. It is also best to have only one parent use these procedures at first until your baby becomes accustomed to them.
5. Over a period of time, you should notice that the breaks between

your baby's crying episodes get longer and longer, and the crying itself also lasts for shorter periods. As this happens, spend more and more time touching your baby. Always remember to stop touching him the second the crying starts again.

6. As you see a decrease in the amount of crying, then increase the number of times that you touch your baby. You can then begin to carry your baby around and talk to him, but be prepared to place the baby gently on the floor and to stop your physical interaction with him the second the crying starts again.

Do not give up on these procedures until you have tried them consistently at least three times a day on three consecutive days. Follow these procedures as carefully as you possibly can. The parent who has the most patience should be the one to try these procedures initially. Do not encourage visiting from your relatives or friends during these three days, so that you have fewer distractions.

From *Little People: A Commonsense Guide to Child Rearing* (3rd ed.) by Edward R. Christophersen. Published by Westport Publishers, Inc., Kansas City, MO.

Ex-colicky Babies

Colic is inconsolable, excessive crying in babies between two weeks and three months of age. There is little, behaviorally, that can be done to treat colic before three months of age. The following recommendations are suggested for dealing with babies over four months of age.

1. *Physical contact.* Babies need a great deal of brief, nonverbal physical contact from their parents (in addition to the verbal and physical contact already being provided). This contact should take the form of touching the head, patting the back, or rubbing the tummy and back whenever the infant is not fussing. This should be done at least 100 times a day, in addition to any routine caregiving activities. These brief contacts are definitely preferable to carrying your baby.
2. *Feedings.* Feedings should be limited to every four hours, with no attempts to feed in between. The baby should be completely awake prior to a feeding, and the time should be limited to no more than twenty minutes for each feeding. The night feeding should be the first feeding to be dropped.
3. *Exercise.* Babies, like adults, need exercise. There are obvious limitations, of course, on the kinds of exercise a baby can engage in. Any activity (like playing on a blanket or bouncing in a walker) that involves exercise should therefore be encouraged.
4. *Sleeping.* Often babies who have exhibited colic have not been on a schedule of any kind. Therefore, once regular feedings and exercise schedules have been established, the baby needs to be put on a fairly rigid sleeping schedule. After all reasonable attempts to calm or entertain a baby have been unsuccessful, she should be put to bed and left alone to fall asleep. Your baby should not be consoled to sleep at any time. Parents usually have to devise a coping strategy to help them deal with the baby's excessive crying. Some take a shower or shampoo their hair. Others have tried ear plugs or Walkman-type radios. Even though it may be hard to do, the baby's room should not be entered for any reason short of a bona fide emergency. If it is necessary to go into the crying

baby's room, do not turn on the light, do not talk to her, and do not pick her up.

5. *Bowel functioning.* Any constipation or passage of hard dry stools should be reported to your baby's health care provider. Constipation should not be left untreated, but do not try to treat it with home remedies.

6. *Success.* When successfully treated, ex-colicky babies will sleep for longer periods of time, eat more at each feeding, and generally feel much better. Babies with colic take a hugh emotional toll on their parents; for this reason, we recommend that ex-colicky babies be seen more frequently by their pediatricians for follow-up after the colicky behavior has been resolved.

From *Little People: A Commonsense Guide to Child Rearing* (3rd ed.) by Edward R. Christophersen. Published by Westport Publishers, Inc., Kansas City, MO.

Time-In

By their very dependent nature, newborns and young infants require a lot of physical contact from their parents. As they get older and their demand characteristics change, parents usually touch their children much less. By the time children are four years old, they are usually toilet trained, can get dressed and undressed themselves, can feed themselves, and can bathe themselves. Thus, if parents don't conscientiously put forth an effort to maintain a great deal of physical contact with their child, he or she will be touched much less than they did at earlier ages. There are several things that parents can do to help offset these natural changes.

1. *Physical proximity.* During boring or distracting activities, place your child close to you where it is easy to reach him. At dinner, in the car, in a restaurant, when you have company, or when you are in a shopping mall, keep your child near you so that physical contact requires little, if any, additional effort on your part.
2. *Physical contact.* Frequent and brief (one or two seconds) nonverbal physical contact will do more to teach your child that you love him than anything else that you can do. Discipline yourself to touch your child at least fifty times each day for one or two seconds—touch him anytime that he is not doing something wrong or something that you disapprove of.
3. *Verbal reprimands.* Children don't have the verbal skills that adults do. Adults often send messages that are misunderstood by children, who may interpret verbal reprimands, nagging, pleading, and yelling as signs that their parents do not like them. Always keep in mind the old expression, "If you don't have anything nice to say, don't say anything at all."
4. *Nonverbal contact.* Try to make most of your physical contact with children nonverbal. With young children, physical contact usually has a calming effect, whereas verbal praise, questioning, or general comments may only interrupt what your child was doing.
5. *Independent play.* Children need to have time to themselves—time when they can play, put things into their mouths, or stare into space. Generally, children don't do nearly as well when their par-

ents carry them around much of the time and constantly try to entertain them. Keep in mind that, although your baby may fuss when frustrated, she will never learn to deal with frustration if you are always there to help her out. Give children enough freedom to explore the environment on their own, and they will learn skills that they can use the rest of their lives.

Remember:

Children need lots of brief, non-verbal physical contact.
If you don't have anything nice to say, don't say anything at all.

From *Little People: A Commonsense Guide to Child Rearing* (3rd ed.) by Edward R. Christophersen. Published by Westport Publishers, Inc., Kansas City, MO.

Using Time-Out
for Behavior Problems

A. Preparations:

1. Purchase a small portable kitchen timer.
2. Select a place for time-out. This could be a chair in the hallway, kitchen, or corner of a room. It needs to be a dull place (*not* your child's bedroom) where your child cannot view the TV or play with toys. It should *not* be a dark, scary, or dangerous place—the aim is to remove your child to a place where not much is happening, *not* to make him feel afraid.
3. Discuss with your spouse which behaviors will result in time-out. Consistency is very important.

B. Practicing (if your child is three or older):

1. Before using time-out for discipline, you should practice using it with your child at a pleasant time.
2. Tell your child there are two rules when in time-out:
   a. The timer will start only after he is quiet. Ask your child what would happen if he talks or makes noises when in time-out. He should say the timer will be reset or something similar. If he does not say this, remind him of the rule.
   b. If he gets off the chair before the timer rings, you will give him *one* hard spank and place him back in the chair. Ask your child if he wants to get off the chair and get one hard spank to learn this rule.
3. After explaining the rules and checking out your child's understanding of the rules, go through the steps under "C" below. Tell your child you are "pretending" this time.
4. Mention to your child you will be using this technique instead of spanking, yelling, or threatening.

C. Procedures:

1. Following an inappropriate behavior, describe what your child did in as few words as possible. For example, say "Time-out for

151

hitting." Say this calmly and only once. Do not lose your temper or begin nagging. If your child has problems getting to the chair quickly, guide him with as little effort as needed. This can range from leading him part way by the hand to carrying him all the way to the chair. If you have to carry him, hold him facing away from you.

2. Practice with two-second time-outs initially, until you are certain the child understands he must be quiet in order to get up. Gradually increase the length of time he must sit. After a week or so, when you should be using time-outs that are at least a minute long, begin to use the timer to signal the end of time-out.

3. The rule of thumb is a maximum of one minute of quiet time-out for each year of age. A two-year-old would have two minutes; a three-year-old, three minutes; and a five-year-old, five minutes. For children five years and above, five minutes remains the maximum amount of time. If your child makes noises, screams, or cries, reset the timer. Do this *each* time the child makes any noises. If your child gets off the chair before the time is up, give him *one* hard spank on the bottom, replace him on the chair, and reset the timer. Do this *each* time the child gets off the chair.

4. After your child has been quiet and seated for the required amount of time, the timer will ring. Walk over to him, place your hand on his back, and simply say "O.K." Apply gentle pressure to his back with your hand for a second to let him know it's all right to get up now.

5. After a time-out period, your child should start with a "clean slate." Do not discuss, remind, or nag about what the child did wrong. Within five minutes after time-out, look for and praise good behavior. It's wise to take your child to a different part of the house and start him in a new activity. (Remember, catch 'em being good.)

Things to check when time-out doesn't work:

1. Be sure you are not warning your child one (or more) times before sending her to the time-out chair. Warnings only teach your child that she can misbehave at least once (or more) before you'll use time-out. Warnings make children's behavior worse, not better.

2. All adults who are responsible for disciplining your child at home should be using the time-out chair. You should agree when and for

what behaviors to send your child to time-out. (You will want new sitters, visiting friends, and relatives to read and discuss the time-out guidelines.)

3. To maximize the effectiveness of time-out, you must make the rest of the day ("time-in") pleasant for your child. Remember to let your child know when she is well behaved rather than taking good behavior for granted. Most children would prefer to have you put them in time-out than ignore them completely.

4. Your child may say "Going to the chair doesn't bother me," or "I like time-out." Don't fall for this trick. Many children try to convince their parents that time-out is fun and therefore not working. You should notice over time that the problem behaviors for which you use time-out occur less often.

5. When you first begin using time-out, your child may act like time-out is a "game." She may put herself in time-out or ask to go there. If this happens, give your child what she wants—that is, put her in time-out and require her to sit quietly for the required amount of time. She will soon learn that time-out is not a game. Your child may also laugh or giggle when being placed in time-out or while in time-out. Although this may aggravate you, it is important for you to ignore her completely when she is in time-out.

6. You may feel the need to punish your child for doing something inappropriate in the chair (for example, cursing or spitting). However, it is very important to ignore your child when she behaves badly in time-out. This will teach her that such "attention-getting" strategies will *not* work. If your child curses when out of the chair (and it bothers you), be sure to put her in time-out.

7. TV, radio, or a nice view out the window can make time-out more tolerable and prolong the length of time your child must stay in the chair by encouraging her to talk. Try to minimize such distractions.

8. You must use time-out for major as well as minor behavior problems. Parents have a tendency to feel that time-out is not enough of a punishment for big things. Consistency is most important for time-out to work for big and small problems.

9. Be certain that your child is aware of the rules that, if broken, result in time-out. Frequently, parents will establish a new rule ("Don't touch the new stereo") without telling their children. When children unwittingly break the new rule they don't under-

stand why they are being put in time-out.

10. Review the time-out guidelines to make certain you are following the recommendations.

When your child is in time-out:

    a. Don't look at him.

    b. Don't talk to him.

    c. Don't talk about him.

    d. Don't act angry.

    e. Do remain calm.

    f. Do follow the written guidelines.

    g. Do find something to do (read magazine, phone someone) when your child is crying and talking in time-out.

    h. He should be able to see you.

    i. He should be able to tell you're not mad.

    j. He should be able to see what he's missing.

From *Little People: A Commonsense Guide to Child Rearing* (3rd ed.) by Edward R. Christophersen. Published by Westport Publishers, Inc., Kansas City, MO.

Discipline for Toddlers

Time-out for toddlers involves placing your child in his playpen for a short period of time following each occurrence of a negative behavior. This procedure has been effective in reducing problem behaviors such as tantrums, hitting and other aggressive acts, failure to follow directions, and biting. Parents have found this method works much better than spanking, yelling, and threatening children. It is most appropriate for children ages nine months through two years.

A. Preparations:

1. A place for time-out should be selected, such as your child's playpen. It needs to be a dull place, but *not* a dark, scary, or dangerous one. The aim is to remove the child to a place where not much is happening, *not* to make the child afraid.
2. Discuss with your spouse which behaviors will result in time-out.

B. Procedures:

1. Following the negative behavior, say to the child "Time-out for hitting." Say this calmly; no screaming, talking angrily, or nagging. Carry the child to the playpen, facing away from you and without talking to him.
2. When the child is in the playpen, wait until he has stopped crying for about two to five seconds. Before your child has stopped crying, *do not* look at him, talk to him, or talk about him. After he is finally quiet, just go over to the playpen, pick him up without saying a word, and set him on the floor near some of his toys. Do not reprimand him or mention what he did wrong. Do not carry him around and console him.
3. After each time-out episode, toddlers should start out with a "clean slate." No discussion, nagging, threatening, or reminding is necessary. At the first opportunity, look for and praise positive behaviors. Catch 'em being good!

C. Summary of the rules:

a. Decide about behaviors you will use time-out for ahead of time.

b. Don't leave your child in time-out and forget about him.

c. Don't nag, scold, or talk to your child when he's in time-out (all family members should follow this rule).

d. Remain calm, particularly when your child is being testy.

e. Don't use time-out for every problem.

From *Little People: A Commonsense Guide to Child Rearing* (3rd ed.) by Edward R. Christophersen. Published by Westport Publishers, Inc., Kansas City, MO.

Cognitive Development in the Toddler and Preschooler as it Relates to Discipline

Children who are seven years of age or younger are at the "pre-abstract level of cognitive development," which means they are unable to deal with abstractions, such as reasoning. If a parent tells her three-year-old daughter, Jennifer, not to go into the street because there are cars and she might get hit and be hurt, Jennifer may be perfectly capable of repeating such an instruction back to her mom and dad, but that is where her ability ends. It is extremely unlikely that she will be able to actually do what her parent instructs her to do.

Because reasoning with young children doesn't work, it usually results in repeating the instruction over and over again, and using threats and nagging, such as "If I have to tell you one more time," or "If I've told you once, I've told you a hundred times." Her parent ends up telling her the same thing over and over again because Jennifer is unable to comply with the instruction, due to her level of cognitive development. When Mom has to repeat the instruction continually, she may begin to believe that Jennifer is openly defying her, and Mom begins to feel frustrated and/or angry. Jennifer, unable to comply, begins to feel that Mom does not like her because she gives threats and yells at her. Over time, repeated attempts to reason with a child can result in lowering the child's self-esteem. As this process goes on, day after day, the parent gets more and more frustrated and the child develops a very poor self-image.

Children learn through repetition. They must have the opportunity to practice the same thing over and over again. If Jennifer needs to be taught not to go into the street, she must be shown this lesson over and over again. Every time that Jennifer goes near the street, she needs to be disciplined, in an unemotional way. Every

157

time that she starts to go toward the street, but stops short of doing so, she needs to be praised. After Jennifer has experienced twenty or thirty trips towards the street, with some resulting in discipline and some in praise, she will learn from the contrast to stay out of the street.

Parents cannot tell small children once not to do something and realistically expect the child never to do it again. Parents need to understand that teaching involves many repetitions before something is learned and that children must do something both the right way and the wrong way many times before they learn to do it right consistently. Rather than becoming frustrated because learning takes place over a long period of time, parents should understand that they are in the process of teaching their child an important skill. The more times the child can experience the contrast between what happens when something is done the right way and when it is done the wrong way, the quicker and more thoroughly the child will learn what the right way is.

From *Little People: A Commonsense Guide to Child Rearing* (3rd ed.) by Edward R. Christophersen. Published by Westport Publishers, Inc., Kansas City, MO.

Teaching Independent Play

Teaching independent play is a very slow process, but well worth the time and effort. This is not accomplished overnight; it is gradually accomplished. The age of your child will determine what type of activities you will use to increase his attention span. For toddlers, playing quietly by themselves is a good behavior to use. For older, school age children, homework, reading, etc., can be used. Select a behavior or several behaviors that your child likes when you first begin.

1. Determine how long your child is now playing or engaging in any specific behavior (coloring, playing quietly, reading). This may be a very short time (one to five minutes).
2. Pick a time to work on increasing his attention span each day. Your child will need the structure of a specific time each and every day to make the process easier.
3. You will want to begin by instructing your child to engage in the behavior you have chosen (for example, playing quietly) for an amount of time you feel certain he can manage (maybe five minutes). Set a portable kitchen timer for that amount of time.
4. Give your child very brief love pats (you don't want to distract him) as often as possible during this time.
5. Gradually increase the time, though the amount will depend on your child. Try three or four days at each time to begin with. You may need to stay on one time length for more than three to four days, depending on your child's progress. Don't lengthen the time until your child is doing well at the shorter period.
6. If your child is enjoying these quiet types of activities at any other time during the day, be sure to give him lots of physical contact.
7. If your child has tantrums before or during the time you are working on this behavior, place him in time-out. After the time-out is over, instruct him again to engage in the activity. Praise getting started and trying. Make this as pleasant as possible but do not give in to the tantrum by allowing your child to get out of working for the specified time.

159

8. Equally important is *modeling* the kind of behavior you expect your child to exhibit. For example, if you would like your child to read more, it's very important that he see you enjoying reading. Don't make the mistake of "waiting 'til the kids are in bed" to do your reading.

9. You will have to provide praise and recognition for your child's appropriate behavior as long as he resides at home.

From *Little People: A Commonsense Guide to Child Rearing* (3rd ed.) by Edward R. Christophersen. Published by Westport Publishers, Inc., Kansas City, MO.

Grounding as a Method of Discipline

Grounding is a method of discipline that may be used to teach your child the consequences of breaking rules (inappropriate behavior). It is not a substitute for time-out; it should be used for more serious offenses. Grounding also provides your child with an opportunity to learn how to do various jobs around your home and receive your instructive feedback. The following instructions describe how to use grounding.

1. Sit down with your child at a pleasant time and develop a list of at least ten jobs that need to be done regularly around the house. The individual jobs should be approximately equal in difficulty and amount of time required to complete. Be sure your child is physically capable of doing each job. Examples of such jobs are washing the kitchen floor, cleaning the bathroom, sweeping out the garage, or vacuuming the living room and dining room.

2. Each job should be written on a separate index card with a detailed description of what is required to complete the job correctly. For example:
   Wash kitchen floor. The floor should be swept clean first. Remove all movable pieces of furniture. Fill a bucket with warm soapy water, wash the floor with a clean rag, squeezed dry. Dry the floor with a clean, dry rag. Replace the furniture that was moved.

3. Explain to your child that when she has broken a rule (for example, by not returning home from school on time), one or more job cards will be assigned. The child will randomly select the assigned number of cards from the prewritten job cards. Until the assigned number of jobs described on the cards are completed correctly, she will be grounded.

4. Being grounded means:
   a. Attending school
   b. Performing required chores
   c. Following house rules
   d. No television

161

  e. Staying in own room unless eating meals, working on chores, or attending school

  f. No telephone calls

  g. No record player, radio, etc.

  h. No video games or other games or toys

  i. No bike riding

  j. No friends over or going to friends' houses

  k. No snacks

  l. No outside social activities (movies, going out to dinner)

5. Being grounded does *not* mean:

  a. Nagging

  b. Reminding about jobs to be done

  c. Discussing the grounding

  d. Explaining the rules

6. When the jobs are completed, you should check to be sure that they have been done correctly. Praise your child for completing the chores correctly and, thus, ending the grounding. If a job is not completed correctly, review the job description and provide feedback on parts done correctly vs. incorrectly. Without nagging, instruct your child to redo the incorrect tasks in order to end the grounding.

7. Your child determines how long she is to be grounded. The grounding only lasts as longs as it takes to complete the assigned jobs—it could last from fifteen minutes to a day or longer.

8. If the grounding seems to be lasting an excessively long time, check to be sure that your child's life is dull enough during the grounding. Make sure you are not providing a lot of attention in the form of nagging, etc.

9. Grounding is effective when your child follows the rules more often and is aware of the consequences of breaking them.

10. Be sure you have a baby-sitter available on short notice in case your child is grounded and unable to accompany you on a planned family outing.

From *Little People: A Commonsense Guide to Child Rearing* (3rd ed.) by Edward R. Christophersen. Published by Westport Publishers, Inc., Kansas City, MO.

Behavior Problems in Public Places

Taking children to restaurants and grocery, discount, and department stores can be both fun and educational for them. In order to make trips to these public places more enjoyable, begin by taking numerous "training trips." These are best described as short trips made for the sole purpose of teaching appropriate store behaviors.

A. Training trips:

1. Trips should not exceed fifteen minutes and could be only five minutes.
2. Choose a time when the store or restaurant is not very busy.
3. Trips should be for teaching, not for shopping or eating.
4. Rules should be stated prior to leaving the house or apartment, as matter-of-factly as possible, and restated immediately prior to entering the "training area." Some suggestions for rules include:
   a. Stay with Mom or Dad. Do not walk away alone.
   b. Do not pick up or touch things without permission from Mom or Dad.
   c. Nothing will be purchased on the trip.
5. Provide your child with a lot of brief, nonverbal, physical contact (at least once every minute or half-minute) for appropriate behaviors. Occasionally offer verbal praise, such as "Mike, you sure are being good," "You're staying right next to Mommy," "Thank you for not picking up any candy," or "It's easier to shop when you don't pick up things."
6. Maintain frequent physical contact with your child. Touch him gently on the back, rough up his hair, or briefly give him a hug, pulling him up next to you.

B. General guidelines:

1. Involve your child in the activity as much as possible. Have him get groceries for you or place them in the cart. Give him educational instructions, such as "Get me the *green* can, please," or

163

"Bring me the *bag* of pretzels, please." Don't forget to say "please" and "thank you" when appropriate.

2. Include your child in pleasant conversation regarding what you're doing ("We're going to make sloppy joes with this hamburger meat. You really like sloppy joes, don't you?").

3. This is also a good time to teach your child about his world ("Bananas grow on trees. What else can you think of that grows on trees?" "All fruits have a skin or cover on them to protect them from rain and from bugs.").

4. By your frequent physical contact, praise, teaching, and pleasant conversation, your child will remain much more interested in the trip. By actually helping you, he will learn that stores are a fun place to visit.

5. If your child breaks one of your rules, immediately make him sit in "time-out." This can be any place that is generally out of the normal flow of foot traffic. In a grocery store, you can just point to one of the tile floor squares and firmly tell your child to sit on that square because he walked away from you. In a restaurant, you can simply turn your child's chair around, or if the restaurant is not very crowded, place him on another chair about three to four feet away from you. As soon as your child is quiet for about one-half to one minute, tell him that it is okay to get up or to turn his chair back to the table.

6. Remember, praise and attention, coupled with firm discipline, are the tools you have with which to teach your child. *Discipline alone will not work.* Using the two together will work to make your trips to stores and restaurants much more enjoyable for both of you. Generally the better your child does at home, the better he'll do in public. When you are having trouble in public, step up your efforts at home.

From *Little People: A Commonsense Guide to Child Rearing* (3rd ed.) by Edward R. Christophersen. Published by Westport Publishers, Inc., Kansas City, MO.

Peer Interaction Skills

There are many children who don't have anyone to play with because they tend to drive other children away. They need a lot of supervised practice in playing nicely with other children. This can be done using the following steps.

1. You must have time-in and time-out well established before you begin trying to teach interaction skills. To begin without a good time-in/time-out base is almost foolhardy.
2. Call another child's parents and invite their child over to your house to play with your child, giving the parent the assurance that you will be monitoring the play activity.
3. The children will be playing inside. Decide ahead of time how long the play will last and convey this to the other child's parents. Don't schedule or plan any other competing activities for yourself—most of your time will be taken up with the children's playing.
4. Monitor the play very closely. Use as much brief, gentle contact (time-in) as you can with your son or daughter whenever they are playing nicely.
5. Be prepared to use time-out as quickly as possible for any objectionable behavior, such as obnoxious talk, refusing to share, or withdrawing from the activity.
6. During your child's time-outs, be prepared to continue the play with the other child so that he isn't sitting doing nothing while your child is in time-out.
7. Don't give your child any benefit of the doubt—if in doubt, time him out.
8. If your child is thoroughly used to time-in and time-out, the first play session should go much better than past play sessions. Begin by having several play session each week.
9. The more experience your child gets playing nicely with other children, the easier this will get for you to handle. After your child is consistently doing well with one child at a time, then you can begin inviting more than one child over. However, don't press

your luck. Work on one child at a time until your child is really good at it.

10. Expect to have to continue monitoring your child very closely during play for a long time to come.

Divorced Parenting

Every year over 1 million children experience parental divorce in our country. Based on current divorce trends, approximately thirty percent of children born in the 1980s will experience a parental divorce before they reach the age of eighteen. It is apparent that divorce and single-parent families have become a way of life in our society.

Many parents who divorce believe they have done irreversible damage to their children because of the parents' permanent separation. However, many of the problems children experience following parental divorce are not due merely to separation form one parent. Recent research indicates that children's adjustment following parental divorce is dependent, to a large extent, on the situation existing after the divorce. Fortunately, parents often have control over many of the post-divorce factors that affect child adjustment. Listed below are recommendations for divorced/divorcing parents that should help minimize the negative effects of divorce on their children.

1. Subject the child to as few changes as possible as a result of the divorce (try to have the child attend the same school, continue to live in the same home, etc.). Of particular importance is consistency in regard to the child's standard of living. For this reason, regular child suport payments are often critical.
2. Don't argue or fight with your ex-spouse in the child's presence. This is perhaps the most important issue related to a child's adjustment following parental divorce. The amount of parental conflict over visitation, support, etc., that the child witnesses following divorce is directly related to their level of adjustment.
3. Consistent discipline is very important. Both parents should use similar age-appropriate discipline techniques with their children. Limits on what is and is not acceptable behavior for the children should also be consistent between the two homes.
4. Don't use the child as a messenger in parental communications. The child should never be asked to communicate messages such as "Tell your dad that he is late with the child support payment."

Children should not be involved in such issues.

5. Don't use the child as a spy. Parents should not ask their child questions about the other parent's life, such as who the other parent is dating.

6. Don't use the child as an ally in parental battles. Trying to get a child to take sides will usually result in worsening the child's relationship with both parents.

7. Don't put down the other parent in front of your child. Remember that your ex-spouse (no matter how much anger you feel toward him or her) is still your child's parent. Whenever possible, it is important for the child to have a loving relationship with both parents.

8. Don't burden the child with personal fears and concerns. Unfortunately, many divorced parents turn to their children for support. This almost always has a negative impact on children and adolescents because they are rarely capable of handling such a stress with without harmful effects. Children have enough difficulty with their own adjustment without the added burden of their parent's problems.

9. It is usually in the child's best interest to have a consistent pattern of visits with the non-custodial parent. Frequent cancellations, long periods of no contact, and sporadic visitation schedules aften have a detrimental effect on children.

10. If major problems develop for the child and/or a parent, seek professional assistance.

Guidelines for telling children about a parental divorce:

1. Be honest and straightforward.
2. Tell your children as soon as a definite decision is reached.
3. Remember that you may need to repeat information.
4. All family members should be present.
5. Describe changes that will occur in detail, especially for younger children (living arrangements, pets, cooking, etc.).
6. For older children, outline steps that have been taken to save the marriage.
7. Emphasize that both parents will continue to love and care for the children.
8. Don't assess blame.

9. Emphasize that the children did not cause the divorce.
10. Encourage your children to ask any questions they may have.

From *Little People: A Commonsense Guide to Child Rearing* (3rd ed.) by Edward R. Christophersen. Published by Westport Publishers, Inc., Kansas City, MO.

Using an Infant Safety Seat (The First Year)

Automobile travel can and should be a safe and pleasant time for you and your baby. This is an excellent time for you to talk to your baby and to teach her how enjoyable automobile travel can be.

1. If both parents are traveling in the car, one adult and the baby should ride in the back seat. The baby should be in an infant safety seat that is connected to the car with the seat belt, positioned so that she rides facing backwards.
2. If one parent is traveling alone with the baby, then the baby should ride in the front seat next to the parent. As described above, the infant safety seat is connected to the car with the seat belt so that the baby rides facing backwards.
3. Any time that your baby is asleep don't disturb her; leave her alone. An infant safety seat is the most comfortable place in the car for your baby to sleep, and you don't have to worry about her safety.
4. Any time that your baby is awake and behaving nicely (either quiet or jabbering, looking around) make sure that you interact with her. In this way, your baby will learn to enjoy automobile travel because you are fun to ride with. You can try singing or humming songs, talking about what you are doing or where you are going ("We're going to go see Nana and Papa"). If your baby has a favorite blanket, place it next to or in the safety seat within her reach.
5. Carry one or two soft, stuffed toys that your baby will learn to associate with quiet travel. It may help to have special quiet riding toys that are played with only in the car. This helps decrease boredom. Remember, your baby's attention span is very short. Don't expect her to keep occupied for more than a couple of minutes or less, particularly early in life.
6. Ignore yelling, screaming, and whining. The instant your baby is quiet, begin talking or singing to her again. You should not yell, scream, or nag. Do not take your baby out of her safety seat be-

cause she is crying. To do so will only teach her to cry more to get you to take her out.

7. Older brothers and sisters should also be expected to behave in the car and to ride with their seat belts fastened correctly. If your baby grows up always riding with a seat belt on, she will not mind having it on at all.

8. By your frequent praise and pleasant conversation, your child will remain interested and busy and will not spend her time crying; she will already have your attention.

9. Many parents like to rest their elbow near the front of the infant safety seat so that they can hold their baby's hand, rearrange her clothing, or play with the baby. Babies like this kind of attention and will ride better in the car if you do this some of the time.

10. If you are on a long trip, periodic rest stops will be necessary to feed your baby, change her diapers, etc. Do not start the habit of taking her out of her infant safety seat when she is crying. Instead, when you know she needs your attention (feeding or diaper change), try to stop before she starts to fuss.

11. If your baby is going to travel in an automobile with other drivers (grandparent, aunt, uncle, baby-sitter, etc.), insist that they use the infant safety seat correctly fastened with the auto seat belt.

12. If you are pleasant and talk and interact with your baby during car rides, she will learn to enjoy both the safety seat and the rides in the car. If you allow her to get accustomed to riding in the car without a safety seat, it will be harder to get her to use one correctly when she gets older.

13. Sometime around nine to twelve months of age, you will need to switch either to a toddler safety seat or change the riding position of the infant safety seat if it is the convertible type. Read the directions that came with the seat or ask your pediatrician or the nurse when to switch to a toddler safety seat. Your child should continue to use a safety seat until she is about eight to ten years old, when she can comfortably see out of the car with just a seat belt on.

14. In all states it is illegal for a child to ride in the front seat of a car without being securely buckled into a safety seat. The reason it's illegal is because to do otherwise is very, very dangerous. Please do what's best for your baby—use a safety seat during *every* car ride.

From *Little People: A Commonsense Guide to Child Rearing* (3rd ed.) by Edward R. Christophersen. Published by Westport Publishers, Inc., Kansas City, MO.

Using an Automobile Car Seat (After the First Year)

Automobile trips can and should be a pleasant time for you and your child. This is an excellent time for pleasant conversation and for teaching your child acceptable and appropriate behavior in the car. Using a car seat also offers the safest mode of travel, even on short trips, for your child.

1. Introduce the car seat to your child as a learning experience, in a calm, matter-of-fact manner. Allow him to touch it and check it out.
2. Remind the child about the rules of behavior *nicely* before the first ride and between rides.
3. Your first rides with the car seat should be short practice rides, perhaps once around the block, to teach your child the expected and acceptable behavior. Point out interesting things that he can see. Make it a positive experience for both of you.
4. Provide your child with a lot of brief, nonverbal physical contact. Also, praise him often for appropriate behaviors ("Mike, you are sitting so quietly in your seat. Daddy is proud of you. You are a good boy."). Young children need specific directions—they cannot make the opposite connection of what is meant by "Quit that!" You cannot praise him too often.
5. Include the child in pleasant conversation ("That was sure a good lunch. You really like hot dogs, don't you? You were a big help to me in the store. Won't it be fun visiting Grandma?").
6. This is also a good time to teach your child about his world ("Jon, see that *big, red* fire truck? Look at how *fast* it is going. What *do* firemen do? The light on the *top* is *red* . . . what else is red?") This needs to be geared to the age of your child.
7. By your frequent praise, teaching, and pleasant conversation, your child will remain interested and busy and will not spend his time trying to get out of the seat. He will give you his frequent attention.
8. Ignore yelling, screaming, and begging to get out of the seat. The

175

instant your child is quiet, praise him for being quiet. You also should not yell, scream, and beg. Remember, remain calm and matter-of-fact. Keep your child busy in conversation and observations of his world. Do not give in and let him out; this only teaches him that yelling, screaming, and begging will finally get Mom or Dad to let him do what he wants.

9. Older siblings should also be expected to behave appropriately. If the young child sees an older sibling climbing or hanging out the window, he will want to become a participant. The older sibling(s) should also be included in the conversation, praise, and teaching.

10. Provide one or two toys that your child associates with quiet play, such as books, stuffed animals, dolls, etc. It may help to have special quiet riding toys that are played with only in the car. This decreases boredom. Remember, the young child's attention span is *very* short. Do not expect him to stay occupied for more than a couple of minutes or less, particularly at the beginning and depending upon his age. Anticipating this will prevent throwing toys, having temper tantrums, crying, or fussing.

11. Immediately after the ride, reward your child with five to ten minutes of your time in an activity that he likes, such as reading a story, playing a game, helping prepare lunch, helping put away the groceries, etc. Do not get into the habit of buying your child favors or presents for his good behavior. He enjoys time with you, which is less expensive and more rewarding for both of you. Remember, catch 'em being good and praise him often.

12. If your child even begins to try to release his seat belt or to climb out of the car seat, immediately tell him "No!" in a firm voice. On your first few trips, which should just be around the block, stop the car if you think that is necessary. Also, state the rule once, clearly, "Do not take off your seat belt" and administer one firm slap on his hands.

13. Remember, without the praise and attention for good behavior in the car, your child will learn nothing from the training trips. The combination of praise and attention, with an occasional hand slap, can and will teach the behavior you want in the car.

14. Your child should continue to use a car seat until he is eight to ten years old and can comfortably see out of the car while wearing a regular seat belt.

15. At about four years of age or at forty pounds, it's time to switch to a federally approved booster seat. These booster seats are specifically designed to protect your child in the event of an accident. *Never* attempt to use a substitute like a pillow or a phone book.

From *Little People: A Commonsense Guide to Child Rearing* (3rd ed.) by Edward R. Christophersen. Published by Westport Publishers, Inc., Kansas City, MO.

Separation Anxiety

The first couple of times that you leave your child with a sitter or drop her off at a day-care center, it will probably be a very emotional experience for you. If you can treat these separations matter-of-factly, your child will learn to separate rather easily, making the whole process much less draining on both of you. Some additional suggestions follow.

1. Do not discuss the separation before it occurs. Doing so will not help, but it may make separating more difficult.
2. Plan ahead so that you can separate quickly. Have all of your child's things together in one bag or her toys out in one place so that you won't drag out the separation.
3. When it comes time to do so, separate as quickly and as matter-of-factly as possible.
4. If separating is hard for you, set up artificial opportunities to practice separating. For example, arrange to drop your child off at a friend or relative's house several additional times each week until you become more proficient at it.
5. When you pick your child up, don't be overly emotional. It's O.K. to act glad to see her, but don't start crying and hugging her excessively—to do so only shows her how hard the separation was for you.
6. Generally the way children handle separation is a direct reflection of how their parents handle it. Do well and your child will do much better.

From *Little People: A Commonsense Guide to Child Rearing* (3rd ed.) by Edward R. Christophersen. Published by Westport Publishers, Inc., Kansas City, MO.

Managing Masturbation in Toddlers

Most young children explore virtually every part of their bodies, which means that they willl inevitably discover that it feels good to touch their genitals. This is very common and should not be cause for parental concern. If this behavior occurs during a bath, while going to the bathroom, or at bedtime, it is perfectly normal. It is unusual for small children to actually masturbate, but they may enjoy rubbing themselves, rocking in a way that places pressure on their genitals, or moving another object, like a blanket, in such a way that they put pressure on their genitals. If you notice that your child is spending a lot of time stimulating herself while with the rest of the family (for example, while watching television, playing board games, or at the dinner table), but not when she is by herself, there are some things that you can do to decrease masturbation.

1. Plan activities during the day that you are reasonably sure your child will enjoy. When your child is busy, particulary when her hands are busy, you will find that there is less of a problem with masturbation.
2. Do not punish your child for masturbation. Do not offer a reward for stopping masturbation, because this is a form of punishment.
3. Explain to your child (when she is masturbating in a public area of your house) that if she wants to "do that," then she should either go to the bathroom or to the bedroom—that it is not something that is done in front of other people. Many parents reprimand their children for picking their noses in front of other people; masturbation should be treated just as matter-of-factly.
4. If you notice your child masturbating in the bathtub, while on the toilet, or in bed at bedtime, ignore it completely. In fact, many toddlers discover that they can get pleasurable sensations from their bodies while they are placed on the toilet for extended periods of time during toilet training.
5. Although it is perfectly normal for toddlers and preschoolers to want to play "doctor" or to play "house," it is not a good idea to

181

let this continue for a long period of time. Young children need frequent supervision for a variety of reasons, only one of which is exploring each other's bodies. Safety is an important reason for monitoring children regularly.

6. One medical reason that children spend a lot of time rubbing themselves is that they have an infection, either a urinary tract infection or, in girls, a vaginal infection. If you notice that your child has redness around the urinary meatus (where they urinate from), has a discharge from the meatus, complains about pain when urinating, begins bedwetting after six months of being dry at night, or has a vaginal discharge, it would be wise to take the child to the pediatrician.

From *Little People: A Commonsense Guide to Child Rearing* (3rd ed.) by Edward R. Christophersen. Published by Westport Publishers, Inc., Kansas City, MO.

Bedtime Problems: Crying

1. Establish a reasonable bedtime or naptime, and under normal day-to-day circumstances put your child to bed at that time every time.
2. About thirty minutes prior to bedtime, start "quiet time," during which your child should engage in quiet activities rather than roughhousing.
3. Go through your regular bedtime routine (bedtime story, drinks, kisses, bathroom, etc.).
4. Have your child in bed at the established time. Tell him goodnight and that you will see him in the morning, turn off the light, leave the room, and close the door (optional). Be sure that there are several soft toys and a blanket in the crib that he can use to comfort himself when he's learning to fall asleep alone (transition objects).
5. Do *not* go back into the room. Your child may cry for a very long time, but if after one or two hours you go in and pick him up, you will teach him that all he has to do is cry for a long time, then Mommy or Daddy will come back in. Your child may also try a variety of different noises, calls, etc., in an effort to get you to give in, but don't fall for these. Stay out of the room.
6. Don't get discouraged—it only takes a few nights.
7. After your child is regularly going to bed without crying for more than a minute or two, it is all right to check on him if he continues to cry in order to make sure nothing is wrong.
8. Follow these suggestions for any bedtime crying to avoid having the bedtime problem recur:
   a. Do not talk to your child after he is down for the night.
   b. Check his diapers as quickly as possible.
   c. If everything is okay, leave the room without saying a word or holding your child.
9. If your child is hospitalized or is seriously ill at home, there is a good chance that he will begin crying at bedtime after the illness, even if he hasn't cried at bedtime for a long time. This is very

common. Wait until after a follow-up visit to the doctor, or until the home illness is over, then begin the bedtime procedures again.

10. Remember that many of the skills that children use in going to bed at night or going back to sleep in the middle of the night can be taught during the day. Do as much of your teaching during the day as possible before beginning the nighttime procedures.

From *Little People: A Commonsense Guide to Child Rearing* (3rd ed.) by Edward R. Christophersen. Published by Westport Publishers, Inc., Kansas City, MO.

Bedtime Problems: Getting out of Bed

1. Establish a reasonable bedtime or naptime, and under normal day-to-day circumstances put your child to bed at that time every time.
2. About thirty minutes prior to bedtime, start "quiet time," during which your child should engage in quiet activities rather than roughhousing, etc.
3. Go through your regular bedtime routine (bedtime story, kisses, drinks, bathroom, etc.).
4. Have your child in bed at the established time. Tell him goodnight and that you will see him in the morning, turn off the light, leave the room, and close the door (optional).
5. Monitor your child *very closely* the first few nights to catch him getting out of bed the instant he gets up.
6. When your child gets up, put him back in bed. Do not talk to him or act angry. Make this as matter-of-fact as possible. Do not tuck him in, soothe him, or even carry him in an affectionate manner.
7. Continue doing this each time he gets up. You may be surprised how often he will get up the first night or two, but don't get discouraged—he is just testing to find out whether or not you really mean it. Don't give up.
8. In the morning, praise your child for staying in bed (if he did) and reward him with something like allowing him to choose between two different flavored foods for breakfast. If he didn't stay in bed, say nothing.

From *Little People: A Commonsense Guide to Child Rearing* (3rd ed.) by Edward R. Christophersen. Published by Westport Publishers, Inc., Kansas City, MO.

Toilet Training

Long before training is begun, parents can teach readiness skills in a graduated fashion, such as dressing. Children can also be taught to follow one- and two-stage directions and appropriate language about toileting. The understanding and expression of language greatly facilitates the training process. Some guidelines to consider before and during training follow.

1. Training should probably not begin before a child is twenty-four months of age. Children over twenty-four months are more easily and quickly trained than younger children. The efforts necessary to train a younger child cancel out any potential benefit and may create unnecessary conflict.
2. Children learn much by observing and imitating their parents. They can occasionally accompany their parents to the bathroom. Parents can use their own preferred toileting vocabulary to describe the elimination process. The child will begin to associate his own elimination process with the appropriate location for that process to occur.
3. Children should not be required to sit on the potty for extended periods. Five minutes is sufficient. Adults do not eliminate on command, and this should not be expected of children.
4. Children can be placed on the potty at times when elimination is likely to occur, such as after a meal.
5. As much as possible the training process needs to be pleasant for both children and parents. Physical punishment definitely has no place in the training process. Punishment does not teach, and the resulting negative side effects can create unnecessary parent-child conflicts. Praise for appropriate toileting can help to motivate the child.

From *Little People: A Commonsense Guide to Child Rearing* (3rd ed.) by Edward R. Christophersen. Published by Westport Publishers, Inc., Kansas City, MO.

Mealtime Problems: Misbehaving

Mealtimes should not only be pleasant family times, but also a time when you teach your child the kind of manners and behavior that you want her to exhibit when eating. If you allow your child to misbehave during mealtimes at home, the same thing will happen when you go out or have company. "Company manners" can only be taught to your child during regular meals at home. If you *consistently* follow these procedures, mealtime will not be a problem, and "company manners" and "regular manners" will become one and the same.

1. Establish reasonable rules for your child. For example, you must remain seated, food is chewed with the mouth closed and then swallowed, not spit out, etc. The rules will depend on the age of your child. Discuss this with your health care provider if you feel unsure of yourself.
2. Be sure to praise all appropriate behaviors whenever they occur. You cannot praise too often. Prompt the behaviors you want; this is how you teach your child to behave at mealtime.
3. Teach your child the behaviors you consider acceptable. Once she has exhibited these behaviors, you can be assured she knows the rules. Any infraction of the rules after that should be considered inappropriate.
4. Be sure to include your child in the mealtime conversation. Do not carry on adult conversations for extended periods of time, as this is inviting your child to misbehave at mealtime.
5. If your child breaks a rule, remove her from the table (time-out) and then have her practice the correct behavior.
6. To avoid having a time-out become a game, use it only twice for any misbehavior during a meal. The third time a rule is broken, the meal is over for the child.
7. If your child continues to misbehave, remove her from the table and take away her plate, regardless of how much she has eaten. This should be done matter-of-factly; there is no need to nag

189

about what she has done. This will not hurt your child and will not have to be done often.

8. Do not allow your child to eat or drink anything except water until the next meal.

9. Discipline whining or persistence in asking for snacks by placing your child in time-out.

10. Remind your child of the rules very *nicely* right before the next meal and continue to use the above procedures.

11. Don't forget to praise *all* appropriate behaviors *very* frequently.

12. Set a specific time limit during which food can be eaten and after which the plate will be removed. Purchase and use a portable timer to tell you when mealtime is over.

13. Remember, many of the skills that children use at mealtimes can be taught outside of mealtime. Do as much of your teaching outside of meals as possible.

From *Little People: A Commonsense Guide to Child Rearing* (3rd ed.) by Edward R. Christophersen. Published by Westport Publishers, Inc., Kansas City, MO.

Mealtime Problems: Not Eating/Stalling

1. Mealtimes should be as pleasant as possible. Make sure you do not nag, threaten, or warn during mealtimes. This is an excellent opportunity to teach your children how you want them to behave in a social situation.
2. Include your child in the conversation. Ask him questions about what he did during the day (without interrogating him). Discuss things that you know interest your child.
3. Give your child very small portions, an amount you're sure he will eat. He can always be given more.
4. Praise him when he is eating rather than nagging him to hurry.
5. Set a reasonable time limit for the meal using a portable kitchen timer. When the timer rings, the meal is over and the table should be cleared without any unpleasant comments on your part.
6. Praise appropriate eating skills, such as using utensils properly, sitting quietly, and not playing with food, very frequently.
7. Offer desserts or snacks *only* if your child finished his meal. If you allow him to fill up on snacks between meals, he will not be hungry at mealtimes. Limit snacks. Those that have nutritional value (carrot sticks, raisins, fruits, etc.) are much better than junk foods and will help to teach your child good eating habits.
8. Do not "give in" and allow your child to eat between meals if he did not finish his last meal—to do so will only make your teaching take much longer.
9. You can work on poking and stalling outside of mealtimes, when you don't have the pressure of the meal. Do as much of your training outside of mealtimes as possible.

From *Little People: A Commonsense Guide to Child Rearing* (3rd ed.) by Edward R. Christophersen. Published by Westport Publishers, Inc., Kansas City, MO.

Dressing Problems: Teaching Dressing Skills

Before your child is capable of dressing herself you can begin teaching her the skills she will need. Dressing your child or helping her get dressed can and should be a very pleasant interaction.

1. Praise your child when she tries to put something on (even if it's wrong), and begin teaching her how to do it correctly.
2. Explain briefly what you're doing ("Here's the tag, it belongs in the back"). Later you'll be able to ask her which is the back and she'll show you. Make it fun, but remember to praise any attempts to do things by herself and, later, for successfully accomplishing the task (regardless of how much you helped). Your help should be gradually decreased as your child acquires dressing skills.
3. Set a kitchen timer so your child can learn that the dressing job must be completed within a certain time (such as twenty minutes), then gradually have your child use a clock rather than a timer.
4. Establish a set routine and follow it as consistently as possible. This will make it easier because your child will know what you expect. For example:
   a. Get up at 7:30 a.m.
   b. Go to the bathroom.
   c. Get dressed.
   d. Eat breakfast.
   e. Brush teeth.
   f. Play or go to school.
5. All children get distracted from dressing by other things (siblings, toys, animals, etc.). Establish reasonable rules concerning dressing, discuss these with your health care provider, and then stick to them. Be consistent. For example:
   a. Dressing must be done in the bedroom.
   b. TV cannot be on.
   c. Dressing must be completed before breakfast.

6. Remember to praise staying with the job of getting dressed frequently at first, gradually reducing the frequency of your praise as your child gets better at dressing. For example, at first you should praise each movement involved in putting on a pair of pants. As your child learns each movement, just praise her for correctly putting on her pants.
7. Don't expect your child to learn shoe-tying as readily as she learns the other dressing skills. Children frequently have more difficulty with this, so just have your child put her shoes on, and you tie them until she offers to help and has acquired the necessary manual dexterity. Shoes with velcro closures are much easier for children to open and close—try them.

From *Little People: A Commonsense Guide to Child Rearing* (3rd ed.) by Edward R. Christophersen. Published by Westport Publishers, Inc., Kansas City, MO.

Dressing Problems: Poking and Stalling

1. Make sure your child is capable of completing the task you are asking him to do. Once he has *shown* you he has the skills necessary to dress himself, it is reasonable to expect him to do so within a specific time (twenty minutes) every morning. Preschoolers may occasionally need some assistance.
2. Establish a morning routine, such as get up, go to the bathroom, get dressed, make the bed, eat breakfast, etc. This will help your child know what you expect on a daily basis.
3. Allow your child enough time (twenty to thirty minutes before breakfast) to complete his dressing.
4. Initially, provide a lot of brief, nonverbal physical contact and occasional praise for dressing. "Catch him being good" (dressing appropriately) as often as possible.
5. Ignore stalling—don't nag.
6. Use the time-out chair for each tantrum.
7. Do not allow the TV to be turned on until after the child is completely dressed.
8. Remember to praise *any* appropriate dressing behavior *often*. Check on your child every two to five minutes.
9. Have breakfast ready after the twenty-minute dressing time.
10. If your child is completely dressed by the time the timer rings, *praise* him and have him go eat breakfast. Reward him with ten to fifteen minutes of your time doing whatever he would like to do (play a game, read a story, etc.), either after he gets home from school or immediately if he's a preschooler.
11. If your child did not complete dressing:

    a. Have him stay in his room to complete dressing. If he is not finished before five to ten minutes before he has to leave for school, dress him, but don't talk to him except to give instructions.

    b. Regardless of whether your child finishes dressing two or thirty minutes after the timer has gone off, he was *not* finished in time to eat breakfast. (Although it's terribly hard to send your child to school without breakfast, he won't starve. You will only have to do this once or twice before your child is getting dressed within the allowed amount of time.)

c. You may want to call the school to briefly explain the situation. That way, the school won't be calling you to ask why you didn't provide breakfast for your child.

12. Don't give in, and remember to praise all appropriate dressing behaviors.

From *Little People: A Commonsense Guide to Child Rearing* (3rd ed.) by Edward R. Christophersen. Published by Westport Publishers, Inc., Kansas City, MO.

Thumbsucking

The use of aversive-tasting substances for the treatment of thumbsucking in young children can be quite successful if the treatment procedures are carefully followed.

1. Approximately one week before starting the treatment, begin increasing the number of times that you have brief, nonverbal, physical contact with your child. This may consist of pats on the head, brief back rubs, or roughing up his hair. Do not talk during these contacts.
2. Purchase a bottle of "StopZit" (or a comparable product) at least a couple of days ahead of time, so that you know that it is available when you need it. You should be able to find it at most pharmacies.
3. One or two days before you begin the treatment, discuss the situation with your child (taking no more than two to three minutes), including the fact that he is too old to such his thumb, that other kids are beginning to tease him, and that both his pediatrician and his dentist are concerned about the effect that the thumbsucking has on his teeth.
4. Begin the procedures on a Friday night. Paint the thumb and/or fingers that he sucks immediately prior to bedtime. On Saturday morning, paint the thumb and/or fingers immediately after he awakens. Repeat this procedure every time that he sucks his thumb and/or fingers, continuing for one week after he has stopped the thumbsucking completely.
5. Never reprimand your child about the thumbsucking. Lectures, explanations, and reasoning are forbidden.
6. If the child refuses to have the "StopZit" applied, place him in time-out until he agrees to the application. While he is in time-out, do not interact with him in any way.
7. Keep up the brief, nonverbal, physical contact throughout the treatment procedures and for the next ten years. Refrain from verbal reprimands for the next ten years, too.
8. The treatment of a habit, like thumbsucking, requires a diligent effort on the parent's part, primarily because the child is not engaging in the habit on purpose. That means that there will be

197

times when he is not aware that he is sucking his thumb and he may be upset when you try to apply the "StopZit." It's preferable that you only go through the treatment procedures one time, so follow them religiously and you won't have to repeat them.

9. If your child relapses at some future point, institute exactly the same procedures except for the initial discussion about thumbsucking.

From *Little People: A Commonsense Guide to Child Rearing* (3rd ed.) by Edward R. Christophersen. Published by Westport Publishers, Inc., Kansas City, MO.

About the Author

Dr. Edward R. Christophersen is a clinical psychologist at The Children's Mercy Hospital in Kansas City, Missouri, where he is also Chief of the Behavioral Sciences Section.

For over fifteen years, Dr. Christophersen has lectured on child rearing to prenatal classes and seminars on parenting. He is a frequent lecturer throughout the United States and Canada, addressing both professional and lay audiences. He appears frequently on radio and television programs throughout the country.

Dr. Christophersen has conducted extensive research on child-rearing practices. He is a Fellow of the American Psychological Association and is a member of the American Association for Marriage and Family Therapy. He is the author of over 100 articles appearing in professional journals and popular magazines. He is the author of another book, *Baby Owner's Manual: What to Expect and How to Survive the First Year.*

Dr. Christophersen received a Ph.D. in Developmental and Child Psychology in 1970 from the University of Kansas. He lives with his wife and two children in suburban Kansas City.

The Third Edition
Baby Owner's Manual
Thoroughly Updated and Revised

The arrival of a baby comes with a great deal of excitement, wonder, curiosity, and activity. The nursery may be full of soft, pastel colors, stuffed animals and diapers, but the one thing babies don't bring with them to their new world is an owner's manual.

Dr. Christophersen gives the new baby owner a great deal of comfort and support in dealing with the baby's first year of life. His advice and information is very helpful and often humorous. Dr. Christophersen takes a practical view of babies; they all have fundamental needs of daily maintenance and efficient operation.

Baby Owner's Manual has been extensively revised and updated for this third edition. The importance of touching, participation by the father, and the development of self-quieting skills are new to this edition. For proud parents of a new arrival or those still expecting, no one should operate their new bundle of joy without **Baby Owner's Manual**.

✳ ✳ ✳

In this book, Dr. Christophersen discusses:

Early Bonding

Safety in Nursery and Bath

Cleaning, Bathing, and Grooming

Sleeping Patterns and Fussiness

Feeding

Travel

and many more topics the first-time
parents will want to understand

✳ ✳ ✳

Baby Owner's Manual is recommended by pediatricians, obstetricians, psychologists, teachers, and most of all — by parents.

ISBN 0-933701-31-4 • $7.95

ORDER DIRECT

❏ **YES**, I want _____ copies of
   Little People for $12.95 each
   plus $2 shipping.
❏ **YES**, I want _____ copies of
   Baby Owner's Manual for $8.95
   each plus $2 shipping.

Method of Payment

❏ Check to:

Westport Publishers   **Ship to:** _____
4050 Pennsylvania Ave.   _____
Suite 310
Kansas City, MO 64111   _____
   for $ _____   _____

❏ Charge my credit card   _____
❏ Visa   ❏ MasterCard   _____

Acct. # _____
Exp. Date _____
Signature _____

ORDER DIRECT

❏ **YES**, I want _____ copies of
   Little People for $12.95 each
   plus $2 shipping.
❏ **YES**, I want _____ copies of
   Baby Owner's Manual for $8.95
   each plus $2 shipping.

Method of Payment

❏ Check to:

Westport Publishers   **Ship to:** _____
4050 Pennsylvania Ave.   _____
Suite 310
Kansas City, MO 64111   _____
   for $ _____   _____

❏ Charge my credit card   _____
❏ Visa   ❏ MasterCard

Acct. # _____
Exp. Date _____
Signature _____

Westport Publishers
4050 Pennsylvania Ave.
Suite 310
Kansas City, MO 64111

Westport Publishers
4050 Pennsylvania Ave.
Suite 310
Kansas City, MO 64111

ORDER DIRECT

❏ **YES**, I want _____ copies of
Little People for $12.95 each
plus $2 shipping.
❏ **YES**, I want _____ copies of
Baby Owner's Manual for **$8.95**
each plus $2 shipping.

Method of Payment

❏ Check to:

Westport Publishers
4050 Pennsylvania Ave.
Suite 310
Kansas City, MO 64111
for $ _____

❏ Charge my credit card
❏ Visa   ❏ MasterCard
Acct. # _____
Exp. Date _____
Signature _____

Ship to: _____
_____
_____
_____
_____
_____

ORDER DIRECT

❏ **YES**, I want _____ copies of
Little People for $12.95 each
plus $2 shipping.
❏ **YES**, I want _____ copies of
Baby Owner's Manual for **$8.95**
each plus $2 shipping.

Method of Payment

❏ Check to:

Westport Publishers
4050 Pennsylvania Ave.
Suite 310
Kansas City, MO 64111
for $ _____

❏ Charge my credit card
❏ Visa   ❏ MasterCard
Acct. # _____
Exp. Date _____
Signature _____

Ship to: _____
_____
_____
_____
_____
_____

Westport Publishers
4050 Pennsylvania Ave.
Suite 310
Kansas City, MO 64111

Westport Publishers
4050 Pennsylvania Ave.
Suite 310
Kansas City, MO 64111